THE TRADITION
IN MODERN TIMES

Graduate Liberal Studies Today

Edited by
Charles B. Hands
Loyola College in Maryland

UNIVERSITY
PRESS OF
AMERICA

Lanham • New York • London

Copyright © **1988** by

University Press of America, ® **Inc.**

4720 Boston Way
Lanham, MD 20706

3 Henrietta Street
London WC2E 8LU England

British Cataloging in Publication Information Available

Library of Congress Cataloging-in-Publication Data

The Tradition in modern times : graduate liberal studies today /
edited by Charles B. Hands.
p. cm.
Includes bibliographies.
1. Learning and scholarship—United States. 2. Humanities—United
States. 3. United States—Intellectual life—20th Century.
4. Education, Humanistic—United States. I. Hands, Charles B., 1925–
AZ505.T73   1988
370.11'2'0973—dc 19   88–17232 CIP
ISBN 0–8191–7069–0 (alk. paper)
ISBN 0–8191–7070–4 (pbk. : alk. paper)

To three teachers--two of whom can no longer know of my gratitude--who taught me well and believed in the values which this book embraces.

John T. Frederick
Frank O'Malley
Ernest E. Sandeen

TABLE OF CONTENTS

PREFACE

The second half of the twentieth century has seen the rise of a number of significant innovations in graduate school curriculums. American Studies has become quite respectable, and the introduction into college catalogs of programs that concentrate on contemporary problems associated with, for example, minorities or women or urban life is not uncommon. One of the most impressive innovations is not really an innovation at all; it is, rather, a return to the past, to the idea that the study of the liberal arts at the graduate level--a study that eschews specialization in any one discipline, and encourages, instead, an interdisciplinary approach aimed at showing the interconnectedness of all disciplines--is vital to the future and well-being of a society.

This idea, and the curriculum embodying it, never completely died out at the undergraduate level, of course. Support for it may have been given grudgingly, and it may have received a smaller and smaller share of the credit hours required for an undergraduate degree, but at least it was given lip service by almost all of the better colleges and universities, usually in the form of requiring its students to take, apart from courses in their major fields, a certain number of credits in the humanities, a certain number in the social sciences, a certain number in the physical sciences, and so forth. Sometimes there may have been some confusion and doubt as to whether even this much time needed to be spent on subjects which took valuable time away from "useful" courses, but there was general acquiescence that some sort of core was a good idea.

Such was not the case with graduate education. With the spectacular success of the division of academic labor proposed by the German models at the end of the nineteenth century, graduate programs with a broadly based liberal studies curriculum more or less disappeared from the scene, replaced by programs that emphasized a concentration in one particular subject area.

In addition, graduate education increasingly became "product" oriented. Students expected to make a living out of what they were learning, and getting an education became tantamount to learning a skill or a profession. As a result graduate students tended to be either young, full-time students who moved immediately and smoothly from undergraduate to graduate work, or they were part-time students whose employers were willing to underwrite tuition costs as long as the courses were job-related. In brief, traditional graduate education had little to do with liberal education.

In 1952 Wesleyan University established America's first graduate program aimed specifically at the study of liberal arts. The degree was called a Master of Arts in Liberal Studies (M.A.L.S.), and the curriculum was initially intended to complement and enhance Wesleyan's teacher education program. Some Graduate Liberal Studies programs still have that as a goal, and many Graduate Liberal Studies students are teachers looking for greater expertise in their subject areas. But the concept of Graduate Liberal Studies quickly reverted, at Wesleyan and elsewhere, back to its roots, back to the notion that education ought to concentrate not simply on a subject but on the person. Education, that is to say, ought to prepare one not primarily for the job market but for life, ought to develop and encourage a system of values, a breadth of imagination, an intellectual versatility and resiliency which would enable one to cope with (and shape) a changing and increasingly complex world.

Twenty five years later, in 1975, directors of Graduate Liberal Studies programs from thirteen colleges and universities founded the Association of Graduate Liberal Studies Programs. The purpose of the Association was (and still is) to encourage the spread of programs which would offer students not interested in traditional graduate programs a high-quality graduate degree that was interdisciplinary in nature and non-professional in intent. Today almost a hundred institutions belong to the organization, and member institutions enroll over 7,000 students and boast of over 18,000 graduates.

The enormous growth of Graduate Liberal Studies programs in such a short time seemed to call, finally, for a book which examined the actual experience of students, teachers, and administrators involved in ongoing programs. This book was not to be a "nuts-and-bolts" book, or a "how-to" book. The Association of Graduate Liberal Studies Programs has an annual meeting, part of which is devoted to discussing issues (financial, administrative, recruitment, marketing, whatever) involved with setting up new programs and keeping extant programs healthy. The book was to be, rather, an account of what is actually happening in liberal studies programs at the graduate level today. It was to describe and account for students who were quite different from traditional graduate students and who expected different results from their education, for a radically different curriculum which raised radically different problems of construction and organization, and for a faculty which had to adjust to the demands of teaching interdisciplinary courses on a graduate level to students who as undergraduates may have had no experience with the disciplines involved in the courses.

With one exception, all of the essays included in this book were written specifically for the book by people who are immediately involved in one role or another in Graduate Liberal Studies programs. The essays fall into three categories: the first three essays consider the nature and need for Graduate Liberal Studies in the modern world; the next six essays consider the nature and organization of Graduate Liberal Studies curriculums, the problems of teaching in such curriculums, and the responses of students to the curriculums; the last chapter examines some of the challenges still to be confronted by Graduate Liberal Studies programs, and the directions that some of the programs are likely to take in the future.

I would like to thank the Association of Graduate Liberal Studies Programs for its encouragement and support (particularly its president, Dr. Phyllis O'Callaghan of Georgetown University, who has harassed me less than she should have), Loyola College in Maryland for giving me a summer grant and a sabbatical to help plan the book, Professors Jerry Kohn of the New School for Social Research and Eileen Kennedy of Kean College of New Jersey, who met with me frequently in the early stages of planning to offer their always worthwhile ideas, expertise, and suggestions. I thank, too, the contributors for being so willing to share the insights gained from their years as teachers, students, administrators, and, in general, enthusiastic supporters of the Graduate Liberal Studies concept. Final--and very special-- thanks go to my wife, Fran, who has encouraged me, worked tirelessly with me, and contributed much, much more than she knows to the final product.

Charles B. Hands

LIBERAL LEARNING, RADICAL THINKING
OR
ADAM: THE FIRST LIBERAL LEARNER

When we sit down to hear a speaker, we have a cultural expectation that she or he will start with a little joke or story, often to indicate that the speaker is a person like you or me, showing humor or just plain "folksiness." This linguistic strategy is intended to capture the audience's goodwill with what the rhetoricians of Rome called the *captatio benevolentiae.*

Rhetoric, or the art of speaking in public and influencing an audience, was an integral part of the basic curriculum of education in classical antiquity and the Middle Ages. It constituted, together with grammar and something variously called either logic or dialectic, the fundament of all education, the intersection of the three roads to human knowledge (*tres viae*), the *trivium.* From this basis a system of human knowledge and control over physical reality was constructed which included an additional four paths to understanding: arithmetic, music, geometry and astronomy, jointly called the *quadruvium. Trivium* and *quadrivium* (as it was more commonly called) constituted the *septem artes liberales,* the seven liberal arts.

It is relevant to reflect on the fact that the classical trivium lives on in our culture etymologically in the word "trivial" and socially in a game called "Trivial Pursuit," significantly predicated on a vast array of useless and incidental information together with a specific cultural awareness and an occasional touch of zany humor. Thus, "Trivial Pursuit" may be more telling about the democratization of learning than many a dissertation about education in America.

The transmogrification of the highly respected noun *trivium* into the pejorative adjective "trivial" has an historical and logical basis. Like all good educational ideas, what had been a liberating and useful civic activity for the members of the ruling class in both Greek city states and the early Roman Republic quickly degenerated into sophistry on the one hand and a rigid educational system on the other.

1

In several of Plato's dialogues, Socrates takes on some sophist or other of his time, demonstrating in the process the difference between critical inquiry and mere clever argumentation without substance or moral commitment. In their turn the rhetoricians and grammarians of the Roman Empire handed on to the Middle Ages a system of education that was slavishly imitated without being understood until it culminated, if that is the word, in the arid scholasticism of the late Middle Ages, where the process of learning was rote memorization and where subject matter had indeed become trivial in the negative sense, i.e. irrelevant to the pressing needs of reality.

There was a similar drawback to the meaning of the seven liberal arts inherent in the term liberal--used here not in the polemical, perverted sense in which it is currently employed in the United States, but in its original meaning of liberating and of being fit only for a free person of high social standing. Such a person could afford the luxury of liberal learning, which was defined as any learning not tied to a practical pursuit or future vocation. The antithesis of liberal learning on this level was thus either learning for all or learning for a specific purpose or vocational application.

Liberal learning, in short, was trivial in a new sense: it meant freedom from practical survival pressures for the gentlemen of the upper class; it was elitist, amateurish and without any corresponding idea that in return for the privilege of such an education one ought to be socially accountable. That is not to say that social and moral responsibilities were unknown to the ruling classes of Europe. From the early Roman Republic to the present day, one sign of enlightened self-interest of any ruling class has been the principle of *noblesse oblige,* the need to act (in reality or at least ostensibly) in accord with publicly perceived social needs. But note the assumption behind this notion: that socially responsible, accountable behavior is at the ruling class's discretion, like charity, not an obligation incurred vis-a-vis the bulk of society for having utilized an excessive share of the commonly available resources.

The democratic assumptions in Western nations, as they have developed at least since Locke and Rousseau, are quite different. There the legitimacy of elites and their privileged education rests, like all parts of the social and political contractual system, on the interdependence of mass and elite, rulers and ruled, peoples and governments. Elites are deliberately freed from the pressures of everyday survival in

2

order to attend to social needs nobody else is able or willing to attend to.

Liberal education thus redefined becomes the deliberate choice of society to tolerate, indeed support, for a limited period the relative luxury of a limited number of individuals from quotidian demands in return for their potential future contribution to the commonweal, the social good of all. This democratic redefinition of liberal education implies a right of the people to such future service and an obligation of the elite to render it.

Let me dwell briefly on some aspects of liberal learning as employed here and give an example or two of its social applicability. Definitions, as logicians have told us again and again, are best gained by an indication of what they exclude. Liberal learning regards as significant parts of its exclusionary opposite, in other words as significant parts of illiberal learning, both vocational training for a specific purpose and ideological indoctrination of any sort. While these two kinds of illiberalism by no means exhaust the range of possible opposites, they do indicate some important aspects. They both aim at immediate applicability of the material learned; they already know what they want to use their learning for, and they deliberately and--quite appropriately, given their goals and assumptions--rigorously exclude any consideration of alternatives as distracting and irrelevant. They are fundamentally short-range in their orientation and thus have the lure and fascination of instant, measurable success and gratification. They are, incidentally, hallmarks of the engineering and totalitarian mentalities; they are typical of instrumentalist thinkers whose tolerance for ambiguity is minimal and whose primary aim is short-term control and efficiency.

I do not mean to imply here that a society can or should do completely without such modes of thought and behavior. In fact, I believe a modern technological society has no choice in the matter anymore. The questions are, rather, who provides the corrective alternatives, what are they, and what assumptions do they rest on?

Liberal learning, as I would like to redefine it for today, rests essentially on a set of assumptions that should be made clear since unexamined assumptions proclaimed as true, self-evident, normal or natural are a typical case of illiberal deception, of self and others. One of the assumptions is that, in addition to short-range thinking and action, societies that want to survive and prosper also need long-range goals, aspirations and ideals. Those cannot possibly be the everyday responsibility of decision makers or engineers. They require a different environment to prosper and a mindset significantly at odds with reality as it is normally (whatever that means) perceived.

At stake is the long-range survival and the quality of life not only of individuals or societies but quite possibly of man as a species. Threats to global survival include not only the potential for nuclear holocaust or the destruction of our fragile biosphere because of short-term thinking about military and political supremacy or economic exploitation, but also the potential for an international economic disaster should the seriously unbalanced current international loan structure collapse and with it the semblance of socio-economic stability that now masks massive inequities around the globe.

It is not a question of whether the short-term doers are aware of these issues or not--they are, by and large. The question is, do they have the time and the inclination to attend to them, to think them through, devise reasonable scenarios for addressing them, and then act? The answer is plain and discouraging: They do not. Time pressure and functional differentiation of modern society are only partial answers for that failure. More fundamental is the mindset of the illiberally educated and the illiberally thinking person. Short-range, illiberal thinking essentially accepts reality--social, physical, scientific--as presented in basic schooling, and is opposed to and uncomfortable with the need to constantly critique those notions. Above all, illiberal thinking shies away from a rigorous questioning of the obvious. Liberal learning, on the other hand, is precisely the continuous, persistent questioning of the obvious. This is not some perverse behavior, as the terrible simplifiers of all ages have always maintained; it is rather the assumption that man's knowledge of reality is unreliable, dubious, constantly in need of revision. Introductory psychology and its famous examples of the complexity and unreliablity of human perception demonstrate that notion no less than does the Judeo-Christian idea of the imperfection of man, sometimes referred to as original sin. In fact, some Western thinkers have seen the story of the fall of man in the Old Testament as an apt parable for radical criticism, the obvious requirement for any liberal learning process.

As we are told in the Bible, God, having created

everything, including Adam and Eve, indicated to them that they were to share dominion over creation with him. But he excluded one phenomenon from this perfect union, the tree of knowledge whose fruit was declared inappropriate for the human species. Given this exclusion, anyone who ate from the tree would by that very act call into question the creator and all of creation fundamentally, down to the roots of all being; in short, it meant to question radically, as the Latin derivation of the term radical tells us. *Radix* is the root or basis. Being radical thus means going to the root, getting to the bottom of something. If going to the roots of reality is integral to liberal learning, it would seem to follow that being liberally educated is to be radical by definition.

But the incident in the Garden of Eden is also instructive in another sense. By eating the fruit from the tree of knowledge, man learned to differentiate--between good and evil, himself and God, life and death. Our modern English words critic, critical and criticism derive from the Greek words for judging, deciding between alternatives, in short differentiating.

Eating from the tree of knowledge was thus the first act of radical criticism, Adam the first liberal learner, and the expulsion from paradise the first result of a liberal education. This is to be taken quite seriously and almost literally. One cannot be both liberated and secure, radically critical and naive, aware of long-range needs of the world and satisfied with the way it is run from day to day. The simple, unquestioning, undifferentiated idyllic co-existence of God and man has been sundered forever by Adam's acceptance of the fruit from the hand of Eve. Hence, liberal learning, liberation from prefabricated judgment, is always uncomfortable in its consequences, both for the learner and his society.

Such a learner will not simply accept things as they are but will question them. Questioning often leads to results that are disquieting, whether they reveal the insignificance of man in an infinite universe through science or the morally indefensible acts of a nation in pursuit of its supposedly manifest destiny.

It should not surprise us, therefore, that those who have tried to teach their fellow humans to learn liberally by critiquing radically have often fared poorly at the hands of their contemporaries even though later centuries might have praised their courage. It is no accident that the Athenians forced Socrates to drink the cup of hemlock, that the high

5

priest of the Jews and the Roman local commander collaborated in the execution of Christ, that the Catholic Church decided that Galileo's findings would not be made public to the masses, or that critics of the foreign and domestic policies of a given American administration are immediately labeled unpatriotic. Truly radical critics always do something most people do not want to do--they force us to rethink what we thought we already knew and could take for granted. They thus deprive us of the expectation of normalcy and predictability, which always seems to lead to a hostile reaction on the part of those whose prejudgments are being challenged.

Always remember that the man in Plato's cave allegory, who is gradually led to the light, not only experiences pain during the learning process but also tries to resist actively. Moreover, the doubts and ambiguities of global thinking, the long-range openness to alternative views, are often perceived as a threat to immediate needs and their realization, as we can readily see when we follow the debates between industries and environmentalists, between proponents of nuclear power and those fearful of nuclear waste, and between those who argue for global awareness and those who champion narrow nationalism.

There are, of course, positive sides to liberal learning and radical criticism for the individual and for society; otherwise, they would not have continued as options in the educational experience of the West. The individual derives liberation from the pressures of the here and now, not only by the privileged temporary status of learner but, even more importantly, by being able to perceive, and thus possibly pursue, alternatives to what is seen as an unsatisfactory present.

Radical criticism, after all, opens up the understanding of reality down to its underlying forces or assumptions and thus improves the possibility for positive transformations. It is this hope for an improved society that underlies Plato's theory of education and society as well as Machiavelli's instructions for modern politics; it informs Luther's critique of Catholic orthodoxy as well as Locke's and Jefferson's critiques of absolute monarchy; it lies behind Marx's reading of industrialized societies as well as Freud's investigation of the human psyche.

The list could be readily expanded to include the fundamental questions of the physical world from Pythagoras and Ptolemy to Darwin, Mendel, Watson and Crick, Planck, Einstein, and Hoyle--all of whose hypotheses and possible explanations of natural phenomena have challenged and expanded our naive notions of physical reality and the universe we live in. Indeed, the concept of basic research in the natural sciences is but another translation of radical criticism. No one can doubt that these critics of our modes of perceiving and treating reality have expanded our private horizons while, at the same time, helping to change the world we share, both physically and socially.

The example of the natural sciences also brings into sharp focus the step needed beyond liberal learning and radical criticism, especially in the currently hottest fields, molecular biology and biochemistry. Here we have gone very rapidly and recently from the realm of basic research to the development of applications, from the first insights into the theoretical structure of DNA to the effective and attractive recombinant DNA technique. Initially, the potential dangers of this powerful research tool were quickly pointed out and discussed, but these dangers have since been swept aside by the scientific and economic potential inherent in this new technology. Now, most practitioners of molecular biology, especially those who are socially conscious and liberally educated, will point out that they and their more short-range oriented colleagues do not feel equipped to decide whether what can be done technically should be done morally. These scientists are calling for a moral and social decision which they feel they cannot make as scientists, but which needs to be made for the sake of society as a whole.

Here we touch upon the socially positive and relevant role of liberal education and radical criticism. The expert cannot, one is almost tempted to add "of course" here, be the person one turns to for deciding what is to be done with his expertise. For one thing an expert, as we have all heard before, learns more and more about less and less until he knows everything about nothing. For another, a friend of mine once remarked, experts are people we hire to corroborate decisions we have already made. Put more accurately perhaps, the parameters of judgment used by an expert are often too limited to provide for alternatives or, when alternatives are offered, to accept them as reasonable. Conversely, the very broad, long-range view of a fundamental, radical critic may be too global in itself and require a corrective. The dialectical interaction between the two would seem to offer the best perspective for society.

7

But the liberal learner provides society with another important advantage. In addition to creating alternatives born from radical questioning, she or he understands the specialist's knowledge, and, where necessary, translates it into societally useful terms. If it is true, as has been argued, that we are already well on our way from an industrial to an information society, from short to long-term thinking, from hierarchies to networks, then we will need more and more translators to get us from the unified nation states, with their representative democracy or one party state models, to a global existence based on networks and participatory democracy. That seems to indicate a need not for more experts, whose expertise will be obsolete by the time they have finished their formal education, but for more lifelong liberal learners. Bestsellers proclaim this message, as do top executives of major corporations, even if that message has not yet trickled down to their companies' personnel offices and into their hiring practices.

The decisions that will determine the future and possibly the survival of nations and the human species will not be made on the basis of some specialized expertise but on the kind of critical analysis which is able to define and effectively defend values. That is moral responsibility in the modern context: the fundamental questioning of existing values. Any set of values and the decisions flowing from them are acceptable to the liberal learner only if they have been radically questioned first, and found to be both reasonable and humanly defensible in their application. The apostle Paul seems to have had this in mind when he wrote in his first letter to the Thessalonians, "Prove all things; hold fast that which is good" (1 Thessalonians 5:21). In modern translation that reads roughly: Test everything, but retain only that which, upon critical scrutiny, you feel can be defended as good.

We have thus come full circle in more senses than one. Historically, we are back at the beginnings of Western civilization and its moral and educational precepts, according to which the unexamined life is not worth living. Etymologically, the key terms of the title refer us back to Greece and Rome and Christianity, three basic ingredients of Western history and culture. Being liberally educated means recognizing and appreciating this tradition, testing it and reveling in it without becoming its slave. We constantly need to engage in liberal learning, since we never know enough; in radical criticism, since we can never be sure of what we know; and

8

in discharging our moral responsibility, since without it we could never be liberated nor could our societies be just. Two assumptions stand behind all of these comments, of course, and might as well be made explicit and baldly stated: first, that as humans we have no rights to anything unless we are prepared to understand and accept the social and moral responsibilities corresponding to those rights, and second, that whatever remarks we make are never intended-- as should be self-evident by now--to answer any questions but are intended instead to pose new ones, thus keeping alive the ever-continuing process of liberal learning required of any society hoping to survive by adapting itself to change.

But what may well be a requirement for social survival need not be an essential ingredient of traditional graduate studies. After all, one could argue that graduate work has developed historically and successfully by the continuous division of labor also known as specialization. The expectation that one might combine graduate work with liberal studies as defined above seems, at first, self-contradictory, another futile atempt at squaring the circle. All the more so, as today hardly anyone can reasonably expect to even approximate the ideal of the Renaissance man or well-rounded person, *pace* such rare specimens as Isaac Asimov or Jacob Bronowski. Indeed, their examples show how rare and difficult a gift it is today for anyone to operate with equal felicity in two fields, for instance science and letters. Some years ago, C. P. Snow sparked a lively debate about two supposedly exclusive "cultures," one presumed to be scientific, the other humanist in orientation. Culture in this sense was thought to consist of an inclusive set of basic assumptions, of modes of inquiry and communication--a shared complex of signs and meanings it might have been called later--or of governing paradigms, parameters of thought and behavior. In retrospect it appears Lord Snow had grasped but one particularly prominent aspect of a much more pervasive set of issues and problems. All highly developed industrial societies in the modern period are comprised of not just two but many such "cultures," quite irrespective of their political ideologies or economic systems, by the way. In open societies, such internal pluralism provides major opportunities for creativity, for realms of freedom and mobility of thought and action. In so-called closed societies the price extracted by pluralism is more pronounced, finding expression in competing cultures, whose increasingly specialized modes of perception and operation, whose distinct languages and codes all attempt to dominate, laying claim to privileged, if not exclusive status. But open and closed societies alike have the same basic problems, as do the "cultures" contained in them. In order to make their own information useful, applicable, marketable, or competitive, each culture needs to communicate with others and with the rest of society. This process of information exchange requires cross-cultural communicators or translators.

Such cross-cultural facilitators or translators need not themselves be experts in a narrower or technical sense. They must, however, possess sufficient knowledge to understand the explanations offered by experts in different fields, to decide which aspects of the information provided are important in the other, changed context, and to ask critical questions that might not occur to any expert at all. The literal Latin meaning of the term translation offers a good indication of the operation performed here. To transfer means to carry (*ferre*) over or across (*trans*) some divider or limitation. All translators, be they specialized linguistic or generally cultural translators, carry information across boundaries and, in the process, change it. If something gets lost in the translation, as the Italian saying *Traduttore. Traditore* indicates, or as the assertion that poetry is that which gets lost in translation indicates, then something is also gained. A broadening of perspectives, a setting of the same information into a new context may change the entire valuation considerably. Thus, although one may want to see Shakespeare's plays only in the familiar confines of English literary history and its categories, an entirely new and rather exciting reading of the major plays emerges when one places them in the European context of Baroque theater or reads them as Shakespeare's elaborate struggle with the unresolved, traumatic problem of political succession which Elizabeth I seemed to bequeath to her subjects by her decision to remain unwed. Similarly, the German writer, composer and visual artist E. T. A. Hoffmann has one type of significance in the context of German literature, another in that of European literature in the nineteenth century, especially that of Russia. At best such a widening of perspective, a shift in context, leads to cross-cultural fertilization, to interdisciplinary and cross-disciplinary communication, which in turn promotes the sharing and evaluation not only of information but of the way it is used and the conclusions drawn from it.

Today most leaders of the world of business or academe are aware of the need for such translations and such facilitators but are not quite sure how to foster them except by fostering liberal education on the undergraduate level. At their best, Graduate Liberal Studies programs would seem to be an equally valid vehicle, if not a better one, for creating a mode of thinking, of viewing reality, of approaching and fusing specialized fields of knowledge. Graduate Liberal Studies programs, properly understood, do not stand opposed to specialized fields of knowledge, as is sometimes asserted. Instead, they draw on such specialized modes of information without being subsumed under their categories of thinking, their governing paradigms, or their (erroneous) assumption that they possess or represent a privileged, i.e. "true" view of reality. A Graduate Liberal Studies program can help specialists, by asking them to reach out and make their own specialty fruitful to others while learning from others to ask new and different questions in their own field. It allows students to ask the basic, the radical questions again, the ones no longer asked by the totally initiated and not yet asked by the neophyte. Questions of meaning and purpose, of potential usefulness and hazards, questions that genuinely ask why, not how, something works.

They are the questions someone once said that should be asked by that most important ingredient of any first-rate think-tank: the resident ignoramus. Such a person can be defined as someone who has a good methodological base and a quick mind, who will fearlessly ask the radical questions, insist on equally radical answers, and will not be content with the seemingly professional responses which often are no more than a restatement of the governing paradigm without a full understanding of its implications or its provisional nature. The results of such questioning are often disquieting to professionals and laymen alike, as the fate of Jesus or that of Socrates demonstrates; they can also be most rewarding, as we can see in the case of Bertolt Brecht's legend of the origin of the *Book of Tao-Teh Ching* by Lao Tse. There a simple customs official asks the sage what he is doing, and when told that Lao Tse has found the way to wisdom and the nature of things, he insists that the master write down the results of his meditations for posterity. Combining professional knowledge and expertise with naive and fundamental questions can lead to an understanding not only of important issues but also of the limitations of concepts, fields, and the possibilty of translating between cultures.

A few years ago a course in the Graduate Liberal

Studies program at Wesleyan University made just such a combination of factors its central topic. The course attempted to investigate the scientific and historical bases for Social Darwinism and its political and social consequences in the United States and in Europe, especially in the 1920s and 1930s; this in turn served as the framework for understanding and discussing the critical literary treatment of such thought-patterns and ideas in several novels of the postwar era. This course required preparation for both teacher and students in the history of genetics from Mendel to recombinant DNA and of evolutionary theory from Darwin to the present. It did not require the actual doing of laboratory research that would be expected of a biology student. It used instead, and quite properly so, the results of the specialists to proceed with its questions. It also required and led to contacts between and joint teaching by faculty members from different disciplines whose conversations otherwise might well have remained restricted to campus politics or common hobbies. Thus a biologist, specializing in cell transport problems and teaching genetics, and an historian, specializing in Nazi ideology and teaching reflections of World War II in modern European literature, combined their efforts during the introductory or background stage of the course. In the process many issues were raised, together with some consciousness, from which both sides benefited. They included the question of how much specialized knowledge was required to provide a professionally responsible overview of the history of genetics and its present central research issues. They raised the question of how comparable the arguments of American eugenicists were to those of the Nazi racial experts; they compared the assumptions behind U. S. immigration legislation of the 1920s and Nazi racial laws of the 1930s, both based on arguments first provided by eugenicists. From here, the discussions turned to the most recent claims by sociobiologists that genetics is destiny and the counterclaims by social scientists that human culture determines significant portions of human behavior. All of this, and many other questions besides, needed to be explored in order to deal adequately with the central problem of the course, namely the transformation and deformation of scientific thought into models for social and political action, known as Social Darwinism. The well-documented prevalence of Darwinian assumptions in American thought and action had many effects: it raised the question of the effects of transporting a set of theories and assumptions from one field of human endeavor into another, it brought into sharp relief the potential for distortion, and it sharpened the perception of professors and students alike for the continuing presence of apparently superseded and discredited assumptions in our own time. Students would constantly bring clippings from newspapers or magazines reflecting issues dealt with in class, issues that only a few weeks earlier would have escaped their notice altogether. Their vision thus sharpened, the participants in the course turned to postwar novels ranging from science fiction to Wallace Stegner's *Spectator Bird* and Norman Mailer's *The Naked and the Dead* to investigate in the medium of literature the reflections of the issues previously raised.

According to student evaluations, the course was very successful and demonstrated a number of the benefits and risks inherent in a cross-disciplinary course on the Graduate Liberal Studies program level. The course requires some key, overarching questions or issues around which the material and the discussion can be organized. It also needs and benefits from the cooperation of experts in various fields, who must be able and willing to talk to each other and who will find that they profit from the experience. This type of course turns into a major advantage precisely those disparities in student preparation which are often seen as liabilities in more specialized courses. Here it is a major bonus to have a medical doctor and a practicing psychiatrist sitting next to a high school teacher of American history, and a recent undergraduate physics major sitting next to a seasoned English teacher who is specializing in modern American novels. One never has to worry about student participation in class discussion or about slighting one point of view, be it that of a discipline or of an ideology.

The course also demonstrates that cross-cultural, pluralistic communication and learning can, indeed, take place successfully and enjoyably and that the Graduate Liberal Studies program level is highly appropriate for it. Where else could one possibly expect to find such a variety of backgrounds and experiences in a student body? Inter-field communication presupposes, among other things, a predisposition to be challenged beyond one's present limits while also being asked to draw on existing knowledge and expertise. The self-selection operative in many Graduate Liberal Studies programs virtually guarantees the kind of clientele that is ideally suited for the continued exploration of issues based on, but ranging beyond, the confines of limited "cultural" definitions or the short-range practicalities of applied knowledge. Here the big questions can still be asked and pursued, radical questions can be asked without the fear of ridicule, modes of thought can be encouraged that will maximize creativity in responding to the increasing challenges to human survival that short-range instrumentalized thinking fails to address. At their best, such Graduate Liberal Studies program courses represent the ideal community of new Adams: posing the major questions, at the genuine cutting edge of communication and survival. Indeed, one is tempted to ask, if not here -- where? if not now -- when?

Herbert A. Arnold, Ph.D.
Wesleyan University

LIBERAL ARTS AND THE PROFESSIONS

(The following is a talk given at the 1987 Convention of the Association of Graduate Liberal Studies Programs, held at Washington University, St. Louis, Missouri.)

I am honored to be with you this afternoon, and I thank you for giving me this opportunity to speak about something we all know a great deal about, but also something that can be a frequent and unsettled source of concern and anxiety to us. I mean, of course, the position that the Liberal Arts now enjoy in our society and culture, and the position they enjoy--if that is the proper word--in the places where we all work, the universities and colleges of this country. If I say that the Liberal Arts are endangered, I will not surprise you. If I say that they are periodically thought to be of only marginal or peripheral importance to the society in which we live, I will not be bringing news to you. And if I say that the actual importance of the Liberal Arts to that society is nonetheless a profound one and must continually be affirmed and reinforced, I will only be reminding you of something you probably have taken as one of your chief responsibilities. So I think I am here to do no more than to serve as an incentive for all of us to think through these familiar and difficult problems once again. And perhaps as I make this review, I can provide you with a perspective on these problems that is new to you, one that you can take back to your colleagues and students.

I thought I would begin, then, with a passage from *King Lear*, a passage surveying the world of human needs and human wants, a passage evoking a truth about how much, in fact, we can do without but one also asking us to dwell on the cost of surviving on an absolutely minimal level.

After Lear has petulantly misdivided his kingdom, and after he has secured from both of his faithless daughters, Goneril and Regan, the promise that they will maintain, in turn, their father and his retinue of 100 knights, Lear first discovers, painfully, that Goneril wants nothing to do with a retinue she finds "so disordered, so deboshed, and bold/That this our court, infected with their manners,/Shows like a riotous inn. Epicurism and lust/Makes it more like a tavern or a brothel/Than a graced palace." She asks him to reduce the number of his retainers by half, keeping only the wise and sober among them. So Lear, insulted, leaves Goneril, going with his retinue to Regan, there to find solace and comfort, or so he thinks. But she proves even more frigid and inhospitable than her sister, stripping the figure first to 50 and then to five-and-twenty. Then she and Goneril, who has followed Lear to Regan's house, join forces, the better to reduce Lear to absolutely nothing. Caught between them, Lear decides to return to Goneril because she will, after all, allow him 50 knights, twice as many as her sister will accept. But now Goneril changes her offer:

> Hear me, my lord.
> What need you five-and-twenty? ten? or five?
> To follow in a house where twice so many
> Have a command to tend you?
>
> Regan: What need one?

To which Lear plaintively responds:

> O reason not the need! Our basest beggars
> Are in the poorest thing superfluous.
> Allow not nature more than nature needs,
> Man's life is cheap as beast's. Thou art a lady:
> If only to go warm were gorgeous,
> Why, nature needs not what thou gorgeous wear'st,
> Which scarcely keeps thee warm. But, for true need--

There Lear stops, only mentioning but never defining "true need." Yet the dimensions of that need--what we human beings must truly have lest we be less than human--is in part what the play is about. And the great and general subject of the dimensions of human need--what we must have in our culture in order to be truly human--is, I submit to you, the subject of the Liberal Arts as we teach them.

The painful truth of this passage from *King Lear* is that Regan is not entirely wrong. In her cruelty, she recognizes that Lear *can* do without 100, 50, 25, 10, 5 or even one knight. She is correct in saying that of course we can do without a great deal. We can live alone, without anyone or anything, as Lear himself soon proves by living in a state of nature, as an "unaccommodated man," as "a poor, bare, forked animal." But Lear is right, too, in saying that when we "reason the need," when we coldly calculate the minimum necessary for human survival, we will find that life can become all too cheap, that it can quickly be fed, housed and clad and that nature needs neither beauty nor delight to survive. Yet we know that minimal life is not human life, and that life without any beauty and delight is the kind of life we would instantly reject.

What the Liberal Arts teach us and teach our students, then, is about what we have added--what our ancestors have added--to the animal or biological basis in which we are rooted. The incremental, the extra, is what makes us interesting, and anything we can do to improve upon our fundamental biological origins is what we value, and then what we study and teach. So we *are* our retinue, our 100 knights, and we are all the complex adornments and refinements that our historical legacy has given us. That is the richest, the most attractive, part of our humanity.

I know, of course, that I should not begin my talk to you today in this way. I should be more straightforward and uncomplicated at the outset. I should, in fact, be *practical*. Knowing exactly whereof I speak, I should begin by asserting boldly and confidently that the disciplines of the Liberal Arts have a power and an applicability invaluable in our time, that they can solve problems where all other disciplines have failed, and that they possess answers found nowhere else. And yet candor doesn't permit me to be so reckless with my rhetoric, particularly with colleagues and professionals such as yourselves. Like the little boy who couldn't tell a lie, I am not here to be bold, foolishly assertive, and wildly hyperbolic about what I know to be the truth. I am here to remind you of the nature and the fate of a body of knowledge, belief, and attitude that once formed the absolute core of university education and practice and that now feels itself to be distant from that core. I want to remind you of what has happened to a system of moral values and moral imperatives that once lay beneath all great ventures in higher education, values that have now been partially displaced by other imperatives and other realities. As I describe this momentous historical shift, let me say that I have no interest in giving a defensive or pained tone to my remarks. In recounting this history, I want to be objective, not sulky. But at the end I will want to leave you with the feeling that there is a kind of wrong to be righted and that you, being the professionals who know most about this problem, are exactly the people who can help in solving it.

Let me begin by going back to the founding language of that old university that recently celebrated its 350th birthday, Harvard University. In 1636, the General Court of Massachusetts came up with 400 British pounds for "a schoale or colledge" that would serve to train a handful of young men in the classical learning of the time so that they could go forward in their little community of parishioners to spread the word of the Protestant God. As a venture in education, it was, to use a phrase, an "errand into the wilderness." It was all utterly homely, very plain and severe, and there was no football team, indeed no majors or elective courses, nor any technology save ink, and no committees, nor courses in sociology, nor litigation nor tenure nor bureaucracy nor honors courses nor fund-raising. What there was at Harvard then was consistency, centrality and the received Truth. Those who were involved in it had little confusion about what they were doing. And now, as a way of bringing learning to those who need it, it is disappearing. It is a form of higher education that, for good or for ill, has slipped away from our culture.

Let us now move, in my "Rapid Historical Guide through Higher Education," to the nineteenth century, when a great educational thinker, John Henry Cardinal Newman, began to think through what we will call the "modern" problem of defining just what it is that holds a university together. Although Newman hardly spoke for everyone at the time, which was the early 1870s, he set forward a vision of higher education in his book, *The Idea of a University Defined and Illustrated,* that was reflected in the decades after him as students, parents, alumni and administrators pondered the reasons a university had for being. To acquire education, Newman said, was to acquire "the clear, calm, accurate vision and comprehension of all things, as far as the finite mind can embrace them." Isn't that splendid? Isn't that a wonderful mouthful? I luxuriate in the confidence and the boldness with which Newman must have mustered up a sentence like that. Behind such language rests a belief in the rich capacity of the human mind, a human organ that can somehow comprehend all things, and can remain clear and calm while doing so. To Newman, the world, while complex, is not incompatible with the resources of human intelligence.

The nineteenth century, a century of cultural confidence, also had as one of its educational prophets the poet Matthew Arnold, who believed that the business of a university was hardly business, but instead was the "pursuit of perfection," a pursuit after "the best that has been known and said in the world, and thus with the history of the human spirit." Note in Arnold, just as you note in Newman, the unruffled security with which he alludes to things held in common, to the way in which the human being is seen to live in a world harmonious with his abilities, a world that does not dwarf the human but is in keeping with it.

And then look at what people have said about education in our own time. And what is our own time? Well, to begin with, little Harvard College, off there in the wilderness in the seventeenth century with its handful of serious and committed students, has now become some 3,340 universities and colleges in this country. Those institutions graduate some 1.4 million people a year, and they collectively define an industry whose total annual operating budget is about $100 billion. Students in America study everything and anything that can be studied, in places as large as the University of Minnesota, which has 46,000 students on a single campus, and as small as certain liberal arts colleges enrolling less than 300-400. (At Indiana University some 800 students major in "Telecommunications," not a technical subject at all, but something the luster of which is almost entirely owing to the telegenic qualities of Jane Pauley, a graduate of that institution. What kind of strange and painful comedy would be enacted were we now to bring John Henry Cardinal Newman to Indiana, there to meet the 800 telecommunications majors and there to tell them about "the clear, calm, accurate vision and comprehension of all things, as far as the finite mind can embrace them"? Only somebody like Gary Trudeau would be able to picture that kind of weird incompatibility.)

In 1963 the then-President of the University of California, Clark Kerr, coined the term "multiversity" to describe the kind of institution that he found himself guiding. Taking a leaf from Robert Maynard Hutchins, who some years before had said that the modern university is "a series of separate schools and departments held together by a central heating system," Kerr changed the metaphor but not the idea by saying that the university is "a series of individual faculty entrepreneurs held together by a common grievance over parking."

If this is the kind of creature we now have empowered and set in motion to educate people in this country--a creature of giant dimensions and complications, a creature of many articulated parts serving myriad uses and growing ever more powerful by its great appetite to incorporate everything surrounding it--the question we must ask is: what is the soul of this creature and what does it believe? To this question, Frank Rhoades, President of Cornell University, has said that "there is almost no common commitment among faculty members, except to their academic discipline, and there is no agreement as to how we should shape the curriculum or explore the map of human experience." Echoing this kind of self-critical judgment, the former President of Yale University, Bartlett Giamatti, has said that university administrators have been forced to "see themselves as managers first, academics second. They talk about strategy, not vision. Numbers replace rhetoric." What we are hearing, then, from modern university presidents is that the centrality of definition, the consistency of function, and the "common pursuit" of ideals are on their way to extinction in American higher education. What once was our shaping spirit is now no more than our rhetoric.

But need it be all just rhetoric? As universities have, over the decades, been asked to do more, to answer more needs of the community, the state, the nation, as they have been asked to enter into more durable relationships with the public, with industry and with government, have the surrender of a shared purpose and the disappearance of vision been a necessary sacrifice? Have we been *forced* to come to a moment in history when, if truthful, we will say that higher learning in America is no more than the sum of its individual parts, and has no more reason to survive than to be responsive to its many petitioners? The process of education is, after all, expensive--in time, in human emotion, in money. Is it right that such an expensive undertaking have no particular guidance, no gyroscope keeping the respective parts in balance, no idea to which the vast number of participants adhere? And is it right simply to say that our only aim is "excellence," that we should be happy to think that we are doing "better"? What, after all, is this "excellence" and what does it mean to do "better" if the very qualities of "good" have not been defined?

Well, my duty is not just to walk into your lives and assault you with a fistful of tough questions that many of you, I trust, have been puzzling over for quite a few years. Rather it is to enlist you to imagine, along with me, that the answers we must have to make education work for us, and for our children, and for future generations, are not as far away from us as we might fear. If we have educational fragmentation in this country, as I think we do, and if, for many historical reasons, we have lost the firm anchor in religious understanding that defined Harvard in the seventeenth century and the liberal arts colleges of the nineteenth century, I do not think we have to resign ourselves to the scattering and the fragmentation everywhere around us. We can do better.

How, you ask? I think the answer is to look within the educational institutions that we have been building up for year after year in this country and to surprise ourselves with the recognition that we have stored there the answers we need to the question of fragmentation. I don't think we need to develop a new value system, as some have suggested, to make sense of what we are supposed to be doing. We know already.

I mean by this that if there is any one American institution that has been preparing itself to speak to the issue of values, to the issue of what truly is important in a world where there are many contenders for importance, and to the issue of what remains of enduring consequence and what surely is ephemeral, that institution is the university or college. In many respects, those institutions have supplanted the churches of the nation--not with respect to the link with a supreme being and with salvation, but with respect to their being relatively detached citadels of contemplation, places where fundamental claims and fundamental preconceptions can be aired and even occasionally reconciled, where the essential can be distinguished from the useless, the temporary and the insipid. Indeed, the only reason a campus looks like a campus is that the setting is there to remind the citizenry that it is a separate place and that its manner of conducting its affairs is unique. That, of course, is what students feel and are supposed to feel; that is what teachers are supposed to convey; and that is what campus visitors are supposed to absorb and even envy.

At the very center of most campuses stands the Department of Philosophy, and there is taught a history of many of the most memorable attempts to construct systems whereby the apparent confusion of the world can be rendered orderly and understandable. What people find if they take courses in Philosophy (and you and I know this to be a fact) is that their own sense of confusion can be illuminated by seeing it in comparison with the apparent confusion against which earlier philosophers built their systems. *Their*

21

confusion then becomes only relatively painful, and their sense of being especially disadvantaged is ameliorated. The Department of Philosophy will not give anyone a philosophy, but it will give the means to understand how a good one might be built. It does that by showing the glories and the inadequacies of previous attempts.

And if we now, as our second stop, move to the History Department, near the center of almost every campus, we move into the presence of a field of study where everything is at first rendered terribly small and inconsequential because, whatever it is, it is dwarfed by everything else in historical time. But the History Department is also the place where everything gets to be important all over again--and thus made interesting and consequential--because it is remembered and, we hope, described correctly. Without historians we would not know the follies of our predecessors, and their little successes and all their errors, and, in fact, we wouldn't know very much at all and would be made to feel a kind of loneliness. Such loneliness is inappropriate to the human species. So history provides us with company, out of the past. Our current errors turn out to have analogies in that past, and in such similarities there is sweet consolation. We begin to understand what human beings have somehow *always* been doing. Again, I want to say that you and I know this to be a fact.

And if we steer our way to the English Department, or to the German or Italian or French or Spanish Department, we can learn that language both frees us and imprisons us, for as human creatures we must express ourselves as clearly and forcefully as we can, knowing all the while that how we express ourselves gives us away and emphasizes our differences from everyone else in the human tribe. Language, an avenue, is also a prison. That truth, manifest in politics, diplomacy, and economic relations, is taught at the places where we work. Again, these are facts as we know them about the places where we work.

And if we at last move to the Department of Art or of Music or of Drama, we come to the apparently most useless, and therefore the most valuable, of all campus places. They remind us that human beings are not, in the end, machines or worker bees or units of production and consumption, but are the only living things for whom elegance and charm and grace carry any significance whatsoever. Those places are all about the incremental, the extra, the things we have added to our brute substance. They are the places that provide answers to the plaintive cry, "What need one?" Those places tell us that the characteristics of all good human decision and action include an interest in how the finished thing will constitute an addition to the basic and the practical, how that thing will look, how it will feel, how it will *fit*. Each of us carries a sense of beauty, and in the late twentieth century, it is battered. The Fine Arts, as they are taught, remind students how much ugliness we have all had to absorb in our time. That our senses can be reawakened and made fresh again by these disciplines is another kind of consolation. Again, an understood fact about the places where we work.

Saying these things, and praising what the Liberal Arts *can* do, I will not say--because it would be untruthful--that the study of the Liberal Arts will necessarily make people better. I know it doesn't work that way. I know because I go to meetings of the English Department at Stanford where some of my colleagues behave deplorably even though they, just like me, have read all the good books there are to read, some of those books several times over. The Liberal Arts do not make people better, necessarily. But what they do inevitably, and sometimes with a vengeance, is to remind people vividly what it means to do wrong, and to behave foolishly, and to live a shallow and unexamined life. The Liberal Arts are sometimes thought to be "soft" or "easy" or marginal. They aren't. They are cruel because they can shed so much light on so much that we would at times rather forget about ourselves. In that way, they are central (and don't forget, that's the real subject of this gathering, or so I believe) to the business of living a life and trying to behave honorably and decently in that life. No other part of the university has that capacity for cruelty. The Liberal Arts are, in short, our conscience, or shall I say . . . our guilty conscience.

For that reason I must quote the words of Prince Charles of Britain when he spoke at Harvard's birthday. He said, admonishing his host institution, that "we may have forgotten that when all is said and done a good man, as the Greeks would say, is a nobler work than a good technologist." I liked Harvard getting censured that way by the Prince. But his admonition might as well have been directed at thousands of universities and colleges in this country. The real business of higher education is with the deepest formation of people. That formation--and I intentionally am using an old-fashioned word, a crusty and conservative word

23

--is the one thing that it has been doing for a long time, and the one thing that few other institutions even try to do. Everything else, no matter how important and necessary--and I do not for a moment underestimate the importance of high-level scientific research at the post-graduate and post-doctoral level--is secondary. If we do not succeed in putting the most interesting and formidable moral and aesthetic and imaginative challenges to our students, of *any* age, we do not succeed. But *if* we succeed, then we will know what we are doing, and the fragmentation I have spoken about will be reduced. If we can remember these basic facts about the essential mission of the places where we work, and if we can remember to teach those facts to all whom we meet, then we will have done well. If we can keep in mind that the real object of education is to leave a person in the condition of continually asking (and not necessarily answering) questions, and if we can agree with the psychologist B. F. Skinner that "education is what survives when what has been learnt has been forgotten," then we will have nothing to be sorry about. Indeed, when we take the Liberal Arts to the professions, those messages are exactly the ones we should be transmitting.

That, then, seems to be our mission. I speak to you because you are in a good position to know that everything we do need not be directed exclusively to the young, the post-adolescent. If we have something substantial and strong to say, our audience need not be limited to those who were born between 1968 and 1972. Very little in the Liberal Arts is so tightly focussed. I strongly urge all of us to relax into the confident position of knowing that what we have to say awaits a happy reception from those who are already in adult life and who have already finished some considerable part of their lives. I will not say--because it is a cheap shot--that the Liberal Arts are wasted on the young. But I will remind you that some of the most delicate and pregnant issues we as teachers reveal touch people when they have seen much of life directly, and not from afar and only in the imagination. When Tolstoy wrote, he did not direct his work to a youthful audience. Nor did Richard Strauss when he composed his *Four Last Songs.* Nor did Goya when he painted his visions of war. We have an immense audience to reach. Their workaday professions only partially satisfy them. Some of them thrive on thin emotional gruel. And, bless them, they *look* like us and were born when we were born.

Let me end with a story, just as I began with one--

24

from *King Lear*.   At the end of his career, the poet, playwright, essayist and critic W. H. Auden made a statement that has chilled the blood of almost anyone who has read it. Reviewing his many accomplishments, among them some of the best poems we have in English in this century, Auden, thinking of the Second World War, said: "As far as I know, there was not one fewer soldier killed, nor one Jew saved from the ovens, by any of my verses. Poetry has no effect." Who can say that Auden did not know what he was talking about, and who can say that he was wrong?   Neither art itself, nor the understanding and study of art, and neither literature, nor the study of literature, save lives. Bad people can read good books and get worse. We should not look to the arts and the Liberal Arts to do things--such as creating kindness and peace--that nothing else in life has been very successful in doing. But what the Liberal Arts can do is to evoke in us all--including the professional audiences we can and must still teach--a sense of what a life is and what it can be. Don't we, don't they, want to know the answer to that question? Don't we, don't they, want to have the right words at hand so that we may ask ourselves, as pointedly and as gracefully as we can, what our own lives have meant? There are final questions about every life. To be human is to want to ask the fairest questions, neither too mean nor too generous, about our own.

And so, if I were to sum up everything I want to say to you, it would be that the Liberal Arts can give us and anyone we teach the terms and the imaginative understanding that we need to phrase our final questions well.

William M. Chace, Ph.D.
Stanford University

THE USEFUL USELESS

The forces that drive people back to school for graduate study are obviously legion, but for the most part students seem to return because they have professional requirements that need to be satisfied, or because they have the sense that the world has somehow escaped them, or because they have the sense that some sort of vacuum exists in their personal lives. These three forces are not mutually exclusive, of course, but one of them usually predominates, and it is convenient to separate them here. Let me start this essay by dealing very briefly with the professionally oriented students, and then go on to deal at greater length with those who come to Graduate Liberal Studies programs for non-professional reasons.

Traditional graduate programs (as opposed to Graduate Liberal Studies programs) tend to attract people who have a desire or need for greater expertise in a relatively narrow area of study. These students have goals and motives which are pretty clearly defined: they need "this" degree and its accompanying research paraphernalia in order to do "that" thing. An M.B.A. degree may be necessary for advancement up the corporate ladder. School teachers or librarians, quite apart from whatever desire they may have for further knowledge, often need to get a graduate degree within a certain number of years in order to keep doing the same things they have been doing, or they need a certain number of graduate credits in order to qualify for salary increments. Thus, they enter a traditional program in, say, education.

To be sure, the same type of student will sometimes eschew traditional programs and enter non-traditional programs for many of the same reasons. That is to say, unless a specific specialty is required (e.g., school psychologist, credentials for teaching the emotionally disturbed) many of the aforementioned teachers and librarians will enroll in non-traditional programs because they can earn their advancement by taking those "content courses" which will give them a wider range in the classroom, and many business people will enroll because they feel the need for greater breadth to go along with their already solid professional

27

qualifications.

People with no specific professional expertise may also enroll in non-traditional programs with the vague hope of receiving training of some kind. The training they seek is usually not in frankly vocational fields such as business administration or computer programming; people are quite aware that specific programs exist for the teaching of these skills. Indeed, usually the students themselves are not clear as to what type of training they want or to what vocational purposes the "training" of a Graduate Liberal Studies program can be put. They are simply looking for new paths, driven by dissatisfaction with their present activity (or lack thereof), or dissatisfaction with their present economic status. But they do not know what paths are available, and so they usually frame their concerns in general terms, asking what the program will "qualify me to do."

These people clearly ought to be welcomed into the program--given their vagueness there is no place else for them to go--but they ought to be told quite frankly that the program won't "qualify" them to do anything in the narrow sense of the word "qualify," and that Graduate Liberal Studies programs teach no "skill." But they ought also to be told that if the program doesn't do anything to teach them a *skill*, it will usually help them to unleash *talents* that they already possess. A case in point: a panel of eighteen educators appointed by the Association of Medical Colleges to study the state of medical education recently called attention to the critical importance of a good bedside manner and to the failure of medical schools to help their students cultivate one. Dr. Steven Muller, president of The Johns Hopkins University and chairman of the panel, says, "We perceive a continuing erosion of general education for physicians, an erosion that has not been arrested, but is instead accelerating." And he goes on to say, "The present system of general professional education for medicine will become increasingly inadequate unless it is revised." The revision suggested by the panel would take the form of encouraging future physicians to become more involved with liberal studies in order to "help them become more caring individuals."

Such pronouncements may sound absolutely overwhelming (even irrelevant) to the would-be, first-time graduate students who in their wildest dreams do not credit themselves with training or skills comparable to those of a physician. But basically the same point, if on a less exalted level, has been made again and again by students in Graduate Liberal Studies programs. Any number of them have leaped into a program for vague vocational reasons, armed only with the faith that it couldn't hurt them to know more, that perhaps they would discover new directions as they went along, or that in any case a Master's degree in anything would be preferable to no Master's degree at all. And many have had their faith rewarded by the discovery that the broader vision and flexibility provided by the program can open up opportunities they had not previously considered. One of my graduates writes:

> Early in the program I harbored the hope that within this great diversity of ideas I might find myself--decide what I wanted to do when I grew up [she was already in her thirties]. I imagined it would help me to narrow my focus; what it did was broaden my vistas. I was awed by the number of potential careers I could take seriously. But it was years before I fully grasped the impact of this experience or appreciated its long-term benefits.

And another:

> With all the current focus on education for career-hot fields (sure I took a course in word processing) I am more convinced than ever that the broad study of humanities, by which we develop life-enduring values, is ultimately the most neglected and powerful career-preparing discipline.

These students are simply repeating in different terms Dr. Muller's suggestion that further study in those subjects which are not vocationally rooted can be useful in preparing one for a vocation. It is this idea that validates the notion that a Graduate Liberal Studies program can be valuable even to those students who enter with the mistaken hope that it will give them professional training. The idea is not new, of course: Cardinal Newman, in a different context, pointed out years ago that whatever is good is useful. But in the twentieth century, with its emphasis upon specialization, we perhaps need to be reminded of it again.

Having said this, let me spend a bit more time discussing the validity and uses of Graduate Liberal Studies programs for students who approach graduate study with no sense that it will make them better qualified for employment of any kind. Some of these already have an occupation outside the home, are reasonably content with it, or, if they are discontented, are seeking change through means other than Graduate Liberal Studies programs. Some have no particular desire or need to join the outside work force. This group is much more heterogeneous than the group we have been discussing, and they are motivated to undertake graduate study for more diverse reasons. In general, however, they are concerned either with knowing more about what the world is like, or with knowing more about themselves and how they can develop themselves as human beings. They are unanimous in their belief that their workaday world is unable to respond to these concerns.

This belief does not necessarily grow out of a disappointing work experience. Employment either outside or inside the home can be very interesting and rewarding. The job may be "fraught with trouble," but the necessity to respond to that trouble may be the very thing that produces the intellectual stimulation which seems so vital. The increased knowledge of the marketplace that comes from coping with competition, or the insights into the intricacies of a technique or a piece of machinery, or the heightened sensitivity to human nature (and the growth of love) which comes from helping a child to learn and develop, or the new homeowner's newly-learned trick of how to start water flowing through a stopped-up drain, or the satisfaction that comes from helping to provide an atmosphere in which a whole family can be comfortable--any and all of these things lead to a sense of personal gratification and achievement. They attest to the value of the work experience.

Would that everyone's experience in the world were so! Unfortunately, there is also the possibility of frustration. Not all the jobs in the outside world turn out happily. Some are consistently dull and stultifying, or at least not suited to the personality of the worker. Even those jobs that offer occasional variety can have seemingly endless plateaus between the peaks of excitement. Instead of challenge, one can find repetition and ennui, and the longer one is enmeshed in routine, the deeper the rut can become. And as

30

for work inside the home, it is not necessarily better. The sparkling cleanliness of a house can provide a great deal of satisfaction after the polishing is done, but once one has seen one encrusted oven, one has seen one too many, and it is difficult to work up much enthusiasm for the task of cleaning it. There can, of course, be challenge and joy in caring for one's offspring, but as time goes by one can also get the sense not only that the outside world is a long way off, but that it continues to recede year by year and soon may be past recall. A student-parent writes, "Three years of stuffing Pampers into plastic bags and shoveling mush health foods--ground in my Happy Baby Food Grinder--into insatiable little mouths had obliterated any earlier sense of myself as a competent, cultured woman in touch with the world at large."

The point, however, is not whether the work experience is refreshing or suffocating. The point is that whether pleasant or unpleasant it may well fail to answer the concerns of the Graduate Liberal Studies students that I spoke of earlier: the concern with knowing more about the world or about themselves or both. The failure stems from the fact that the two widely diverse work experiences have, paradoxically, the same result: both tend to lead one to become more narrowly focused on the task at hand and less aware of the self and the world in general. The very structure of the curriculum of a Graduate Liberal Studies program (more about this later) works against the tendency toward acquiring tunnel vision. It forces the mind to explore corners of the world and of the self which are inaccessible when one is dealing with the rigors--or boredom--of the job.

The assumption here, of course, is that the would-be student is moved by a passion for a wider vision. The well-springs of such a passion are numerous and difficult to locate. Frequently, I think, the source may lie simply in a particular type of mind. Obviously, one needs a large store of curiosity if he/she is to return to the campus, after years of absence, for reasons which have nothing to do with professional advancement. Obviously, too, a certain amount of "brightness" and self-confidence and willingness to undertake new difficulties is necessary. One also needs a certain zest for intellectual adventure, and an at least dimly perceived fondness for past academic experiences. Elsewhere in this book--both in those portions written by graduates and those written by teachers in Graduate Liberal Studies programs--there is abundant evidence that this remarkable

31

type of mentality is not a rare commodity in Graduate Liberal Studies programs across the country.

But as important as these intellectual qualities are, I rather suspect that greater interest in the nature of the world simply grows out of the rewards--or difficulties--of maturity. Young undergraduates, or young adults new to the marketplace, tend to see life as relatively simple, or at least to judge it in simplistic terms. They may give lip service to the notions of complexity and ambivalence, but they haven't yet seen enough of life to have truly experienced that complexity. The discovery, for example, that marriage presents more and different problems than they had imagined, or that remote abstractions have practical implications, or that a multitude of conflicting outside pressures can lead to conflicting, seemingly non-rational, inner inclinations can be quite surprising, and will often lead the adult to see the world in larger terms. Churchill once said something to the effect that anyone who is not a liberal in youth has no heart, while anyone who does not become a conservative with age has no head. One does not have to agree with Churchill's political persuasions in order to understand the thrust of his remark. Maturity brings change. Maturity brings with it the sense that one has not understood or mastered life to the degree that one had supposed, and the sense that one had not realized the number of things which needed to be understood.

Obviously this realization brings with it a new sense of the value of academics in helping to see the world and the self. The contrast between the way in which undergraduates approach literature (my field) and the way in which mature students approach it is typical of all areas. It is quite possible to teach most undergraduates, even reluctant ones (and many of them are), how to read literature--how to come to a general understanding of what an author is trying to say. It is even possible to get some of them to enjoy the experience (though this is more difficult). A few even like it enough to major in it, though mostly for vocational reasons. But even these few have difficulty, in their immaturity, in weighing what they read. They so frequently lack a clear perception of their own beliefs that they find it difficult to see what differences or similarities exist between the newly offered ideas and those previously held, and thus they give little thought to whether their current conceptions need to be modified in view of this new vision. For undergraduates as a whole, then, literature is at best regarded as a subject that is sometimes pleasant and diverting, but not really relevant to anything, and certainly not relevant to education, which they define mostly in terms of learning a profession (which they equate with a "preparation for life").

Maturity changes all that. One of the truly enjoyable aspects of teaching literature to adults is to watch how differently they approach, say, a love poem. These students not only have experienced love (most of them several times) but experienced it in ways--some joyfully, some bitterly--not available to younger students. They bring a richer background to the poem, and since they bring more to it, they can take more from it. They can vigorously assert its accuracy or its absurdity; they are able to recognize what it contains that is new or are able to see anew things about their lives they had known but forgotten or had known passively rather than passionately. Whatever the response they do not deny that the poem has in some way spoken to them. They have a sense that undergraduates seldom have: a sense that through literature they are in touch with life and are being invited to re-examine it.

The same can be said for other disciplines as well. The student who saw no benefit to be gained from the formal study of the principles of ethics may want to begin to look more closely at the bases for moral action proposed by ancient and/or modern philosophers or theologians when faced with any number of contemporary problems which have ethical dimensions (some grand: euthanasia, abortion, gene-splicing, nuclear warfare; some not-so grand: politics at the office, exaggerations in the resume). Again, the need to make practical political choices or to understand current events may lead to a desire for greater understanding of the structure or workings of political institutions or of the way in which particular political, social, economic, whatever, problems have come into being. Eventually their study should lead to a breaking down of compartments and the perception that ethics and politics and economics and literature do not exist in isolation one from the other. Each impinges on each, and all things become one thing. In any case, just as the confines of the job or the home can produce a need to know more about the world, so can maturity bring with it a greater desire to know more about the world than our more immature interests had dictated.

Maturity also brings with it, incidentally, more of the resources that one needs in order to pursue new investigations in a formal way. Additional income or diminishing familial responsibilities may make at least a modest amount of discretionary money available for tuition payments and bookstore expenses. Equally important, additional money also brings with it a less pragmatic view of the world. In some cases this view is born of the realization that money has not produced what it was fabled to produce. In others it may simply come from the sense of "having it made." Complacency may not set in, but one may at least have less urgency to work toward material goals, and more freedom to turn one's attention to learning more about the nature of the world either directly through formal study or indirectly through such means as increased cultural activity. Frequently the two go hand in hand.

This desire to know more about what the world is like --a desire which I have been citing as one of the major motivations for enrolling in a Graduate Liberal Studies program--is usually accompanied by (is frequently indistinguishable from) the desire to know more about the self or the desire to feel better about one's self. "Feeling better about one's self" is so subjective that it is difficult to define, and certainly difficult to talk about except in the most general terms. But so many of my students talk about the impact of graduate liberal studies on the way they view themselves, that something needs to be said about it. Not all their comments need to be given equal weight. I recall one student (fortunately new to the program) who told me with some pride, and not altogether facetiously, that after only one course he already had achieved a certain status in his neighborhood as a highly competent player of Trival Pursuit. But as misguided a comment (and goal) as this is, there is a point in back of it: the student was saying, however unconsciously, that his broader knowledge had begun to give him a new sense of self-esteem, no matter how limited the area.

There are other areas that are not so limited. Many students have the sense that they can develop--need to develop--feelings and attitudes within themselves which are essential but which their activities in the everyday world do not necessarily help them to develop. Earlier I spoke of how one's occupation, enjoyable or unenjoyable, inside or outside the home, tends to narrow one's vision of the world. In like manner it tends to narrow one's vision of the self. We are accustomed to talking about the world as a rat race or as an area in which our vocations or the necessity of "getting ahead" occupy too much of our lives. We are simply too busy to spend time on ourselves or those around us, and we increasingly rationalize and embrace the notion of "quality time." Even substantial portions of the time that we do give to personal life are spent on what we call social "obligations" or the crises that always seem to crop up unexpectedly. This sense that life is a treadmill leads almost inevitably to the realization--however vague--that the inner growth which is essential to our non-material natures has slowed dangerously. It is the sharp realization that such is the case that leads many students to Graduate Liberal Studies programs.

A student writes, "Immersed in a business environment, I seldom hear people speak of personal growth, flexibility, human kindness. How refreshing to discover that Gardner, Percy, Pynchon are actually concerned with human growth and the potential of life rather than car payments and billable hours." The observation is interesting for several reasons. First it presents his sense that he has "discovered" a new world. But this discovery does not terminate simply in that increased knowledge of the world that I cited earlier as one of the major reasons why students enter a liberal studies program. Because, second, his discovery is immediately followed by a sense of his being "refreshed." That is to say, the vision of a world different from his workaday world produced not only an altered external world, but an altered internal world as well. He talks twice of growth-- "personal growth" and "human growth"; he avows that this growth, which is the growth of the spirit, is superior to the material growth around him; and he implies that the new refreshment is more important than the new vision. The self expanded and he felt better.

Sometimes the expansion of the self results not from the discovery of a larger external world, as in the example just given, but from the discovery that the interior world is more cramped than it needs to be. That is to say, it is just as possible to be hemmed in by the self as it is to be hemmed in by the materiality of the world, by one's job, by one's family. The narrower the world, the narrower one must become in order to be comfortable within it. Similar problems are faced in similar ways, and habitual patterns of behavior get locked in: it is always easier to do things the good old tried-and-true way or to look at the world through eyes that do not change. This stasis tends to make one increasingly conservative and increasingly hostile to movement, especially when that movement is so radical that it calls into question the life style or value system by which one has lived. It is easier to accept the self as it is rather than to revolt against it.

One of my students expressed this notion thusly:

> Having left college just before the changes of the late sixties, I never fully understood the freedoms [students] were demanding. To me, they just lacked self-control . . . I was intolerant of any life-style beyond my own. One of my [graduate] philosophy courses broadened my perspectives considerably. For the first time I examined my values closely enough to wonder if I were out of step with the universe. Rules play a less important role in my life now--as does criticism.

Here the discovery is not that of a broader world. The world, in fact, did not change at all. It was she who changed. She had been "out of step with the universe"; she had been intolerant of other life-styles. Being made aware of this, she grew to fit a world that she saw but was unwilling to recognize. The quotation almost inevitably ends on a note of liberation. Rules and criticism, which had controlled her vision, were now to be relaxed. A new, confident and independent self was to emerge.

If one can gain a new sense of the self through an expanded vision of the world and/or the self, one can sometimes also gain that sense by *not* changing but simply by coming to understand present beliefs better. In our society change seems to be a "given"; to change is to progress, not to change is to regress. Undergraduates, reading stories in which the protagonist remains basically the same despite the conflicts he/she undergoes, are usually disappointed. "Nothing has happened," they complain. Or, in the same general vein, when the theme of the story simply tells them something they already know, they tend to believe that the time spent discovering the theme was time wasted. Mature reflection rejects such notions. A Graduate Liberal Studies student writes, "I don't think my values have changed as a result of this program, but I have discovered the roots of my values and have become better able to articulate them." The problem with "old" truths, that is to say, is that they frequently had been adopted not because of any rational conviction of their truth, but because they once had been presented--and simply accepted--as truth. The old truths were rote truths. To come to this old thing anew, however, and understand its validity is to change the self into a more committed and a more self-aware self.

The mature student, in like manner, may be led to see that just as old truths (though remaining the same) expand when examined from new angles, so, too, can the self (though remaining the same) expand when examined from new angles. The text of *Hamlet*, say, remains the same, but the implications of the text always change. The eighteenth century readers/viewers saw, in their environment, something quite different in *Hamlet* than the nineteenth century people saw in their environment, or the twentieth century person sees in this one. And so with one's inner life. The beliefs may stay the same, but their implications keep expanding as they are held up to different lights. Each time a belief expands, the self of necessity expands with it, and one of the things that graduate liberal studies do is to ask the student to keep critically reviewing the self to see new possibilities.

Ironically, it would seem that one can even develop an expanded sense of self--and a better feeling about one's self --not just through the adoption of new views or through a renewed confidence in old beliefs, but by coming to the point where one can accept one's own doubts. New certainties may not be produced, but old uncertainties can become quite acceptable. "I have never been known as a dogmatic person," one student writes. "*Au contraire*, my problem has often been one of indecision since I could see something of the right in both sides of the argument. I do believe this program has made me more comfortable with feeling that way." More comfortable, perhaps, but not necessarily complacent. Another student says, "Black and white become gray. And gray is not easy." But if it is not easy, it is better. The mature, perceptive adult who enters a Graduate Liberal Studies program for non-vocational reasons is bound to find a somewhat different world and a modified self, or modified vision of the self, at the end of the journey.

Great claims! So great that perhaps it is not inappropriate here to say a few words about what it is in Graduate Liberal Studies programs that make these results almost inevitable. There is a chapter elsewhere in this volume that describes the structures of a variety of Graduate Liberal Studies programs across the country, and there is another chapter which discusses the process involved in the formulation of a program, and I don't want to cover this same ground again here in any detail. Suffice it to suggest that Graduate Liberal Studies programs are "non-traditonal" in part because the core around which the other courses revolve is different from the traditional core.

For one thing the Graduate Liberal Studies core cannot be reduced, as in many English programs, say, to the study of the major, major authors such as Chaucer or Shakespeare, and then, with this core behind them, permit students to fulfill their credit requirements by taking whatever other authors or periods they desire. (I disregard the "how to" courses in methodology, bibliography, and the like, and I make the assumption that at the graduate level traditional students already know how to read a text.) In this structure no particular sequence need be followed--one need not "know" Chaucer in order to read Shakespeare, and contemporary American literature can be studied prior to or simultaneously with English neo-classical literature.

Graduate Liberal Studies cores tend to be different. Though they come in all shapes and sizes, as Dr. David B. House points out later in this volume, they generally consist of a course or a series of courses which are essential to the understanding of those courses which are to follow. It is not so much that the "facts" of the core need to be mastered in order to understand the succeeding courses. It is, rather, that the core encourages the student to employ a host of approaches to a topic rather than the particular approach-- depending on the specialization--encouraged in traditional graduate programs. That is to say, it is the vision, a way of looking at things, that the core hopes to expand. Ideally, each subsequent course will also produce an expanded vision which grows, funnel-fashion, out of the previously expanded vision, so that when the multiple visions are applied to a particular subject the result will be the discovery of broader generalizations and principles and/or a more fully realized sense of the implications and complexities of the subject.

The Graduate Liberal Studies core thus tends to be interdisciplinary. Traditional graduate study has as its goal greater specialization and narrower expertise. Courses tend to deal mainly with the subject matter of a particular discipline, and one gets to know increasingly more about a limited area of the world or of the self. Graduate Liberal Studies, on the other hand, postulates the notion that a true vision of the world and/or the self can come only by seeing the way in which a variety of disciplines impinge upon one

38

another and interact with one another. A study of foreign policy, for example (especially of what some regard as "failed" foreign policy, as in Vietnam or the Near East), would demonstrate that decisions cannot be made on the basis of muscle or politics alone. If one is to arrive at sound policy decisions, one needs to look at an area's economics, history, religion, philosophy, social structures, psychological needs, art, literature, and so forth. This is a grandiose example, perhaps, since few of us need to make foreign policy decisons, but equally cogent examples could be framed with respect to, say, how one votes intelligently, or how one views current social or moral problems, or how one helps to fashion (or renew) a city, a neighborhood, the self, or even how one makes decisions about the apportionment of one's own paycheck.

In short, then, the Graduate Liberal Studies core encourages students to look at the world and the self through constantly changing perspectives, and this changing of the perspectives changes the appearance of the world and/or the self that is being scrutinized. It is the multiplicity of vision that encourages one to be flexible and open--even when openness leads one, perhaps, to stay the same.

Or to put the issue in slightly different terms, education, if it is not to be something resembling vocational training, must look in a number of different directions. It must address itself to understanding the past (cultural heritage), to understanding the present (usually by examining certain themes which underlie or run through the society), and to understanding the self. It is this combination of understandings which helps prepare one to defend present ideas and attitudes rationally arrived at, or helps one to make decisions about the future, either by preparing one for what is likely to come or by preparing one to help influence the future under the assumption that people do have the power consciously to shape future events. This defense of the present or the attempt to consciously shape the future surely, at the very least, involves a knowledge of what choices have been made, what choices are available, what goals and values are desirable, and how a number of disciplines might be brought together to effect those desires. A broad, interdisciplinary core and the studies which proceed from it help lead to a habit of mind which permits people to adapt to, and cope with, the problems--vocational, civic, personal, familial, academic, whatever--which lie in store for

39

them all their lives.

And so we come back full circle to Dr. Muller's remarks about how the inner changes produced by Liberal Studies may lead to "more caring individuals." One is also reminded of the remarks of Admiral Charles R. Lawson, who several years ago was transferred to the Atlantic Fleet after serving some years as Superintendent of the United States Naval Academy in Annapolis. Announcing a major curriculum review (albeit on the undergraduate level) aimed at restoring a "proper balance" between the liberal arts and the sciences, he said that most of the eighteen majors available at the Academy would continue to be in engineering and science, but that the core would be broadened so the midshipmen would "have creative and inquisitive minds."

Surely the bulk of students in my Graduate Liberal Studies program would applaud that notion. One says, "A new awareness was born. New ideals sprouted . . . life grew richer and fuller . . . and the feeling continues." And another, "I feel the degree gave me the courage to . . . rely on my own talents."

Charles B. Hands, Ph.D.
Loyola College in Maryland

VARIETY IN UNITY:
THE DIVERSITY AND SCOPE
OF GRADUATE LIBERAL STUDIES PROGRAMS

Graduate Liberal Studies programs at American colleges and universities overwhelmingly share a unity of purpose and goals: they are essentially interdisciplinary, are designed for an adult part-time college-educated student population, are accessible through courses in the evenings, weekends, or in special formats such as an intensive summer course, and are generally designed explicitly without direct reference to occupational or career interests.

Furthermore, Graduate Liberal Studies programs are devoted to the objectives of liberal education, e.g., developing critical thinking skills, fostering intellectual flexibility, and cultivating an individual's ability to create linkages between diverse areas of human thought from the sciences to literature. This shared purpose of providing liberal education at the graduate level for adult students on a part-time basis tends to obscure the diversity and broad range of program types and styles at different colleges and universities. Because Graduate Liberal Studies programs are still a relatively recent phenomenon in American higher education, they tend to be viewed in terms of their outward structures --by those things such as student population and class scheduling which set them apart from traditional, disciplinary graduate programs--instead of by their internal or curricular structures. That is to say, it is generally the characteristics shared by Graduate Liberal Studies programs that are examined rather than the differences. This limited angle of vision often causes faculty and administrators to overlook the rich variety and scope of Graduate Liberal Studies programs at our colleges and universities or, simply stated, the wealth of creativity that has gone into the development of individual Graduate Liberal Studies programs as they address the question: how can we best achieve the goals of liberal education for adult, part-time students at our institution?

The diversity of Graduate Liberal Studies programs stems from a variety of sources. First, Graduate Liberal Studies programs are not disciplinary-based and are therefore

41

not subject to a "canon" of subject-related expectations. A graduate program in English literature, for example, would probably be expected to offer courses in Shakespeare (even if that were not the main strength of the department) and would plan courses aimed at introducing students to the methods of research in English. The same cannot be said for interdisciplinary Graduate Liberal Studies programs. They are "open" in their design, and the expectations of their creators are less dependent upon a previously articulated concept of how their objectives are best attained.

Second, and perhaps more obvious, Graduate Liberal Studies programs draw upon the programmatic strengths of an institution. Strengths among faculty in specific disciplines and the willingness of faculty to take an active part in designing a Graduate Liberal Studies program clearly have a profound influence on the shape of a program. If an institution has an overall methodological, ideological or curricular approach, this approach, perhaps with some modification, may also be incorporated into a Graduate Liberal Studies program to address the needs and interests of adult students. Similarly, a college or university may, because of its reputation, location, or identity in the community, wish to design a Graduate Liberal Studies program with a specific orientation and perspective.

Third, the exigencies of daily operations of a college or university may have a substantial--if somewhat more mundane--impact on a Graduate Liberal Studies program. Location (rural, suburban, urban), facilities (adequate classroom space, parking, student amenities), financing (competition from other related programs), and political considerations (state or public controls on implementing new degree programs) will all play important roles in the shape of a Graduate Liberal Studies program.

There are a host of ways in which Graduate Liberal Studies programs could be categorized: by their internal structures or curricular designs; by their modes of delivery, such as summer residential, weekend, evening; by their audience; by location; by their public/private status; by whether they require a thesis, etc. Indeed, virtually any grouping of program types is legitimate provided one acknowledges that there are significant overlaps in specific categories. For example, a single program may be viewed as unique because of its curricular structure, its method of delivery, or its student population.

Despite all these possibilities, the most significant

identifying factors of Graduate Liberal Studies programs focus either on curricular structure--the "how" of achieving the goals of liberal education--or on specific formats or modes of delivery (evening, weekend, summer, etc.). Looking at these two broad areas--curricular structure and modes of delivery-- is the most valuable way to identify types of Graduate Liberal Studies programs.

Curricular Approaches

The range of curricular structures of Graduate Liberal Studies programs is so broad that it is virtually impossible to speak of them as a unified group without addressing the great variety amidst the unity. One could confidently state that no two Graduate Liberal Studies programs are alike, and one could also add that this is entirely appropriate. Graduate Liberal Studies programs grow out of the academic perspectives of their institutions and reflect--as well as enhance--those aspects of the college or university that provide it with its own special identity.

When examining Graduate Liberal Studies programs we can identify three broad groupings of curricula: (a) programs which encompass a central programmatic theme, orientation, or perspective; (b) programs which offer students a multidisciplinary core or unifying liberal arts experience followed by electives; and (c) programs that provide students with areas of concentration in specific subjects. Each broad grouping has its advantages and disadvantages, but it is also important to recognize that these broad categorizations overlap and specific Graduate Liberal Studies programs may be combinations of two or even of all three groups.

Programs with a Central
Theme, Orientation, or Perspective

Graduate Liberal Studies programs which have a specific theme, orientation or perspective are usually shaped by the overall goals of the institution. The orientation of the Graduate Liberal Studies program is thus a relatively natural outcome of the overall orientation of the institution. Examples of institutions with pronounced and clearly stated themes or orientations for their Graduate Liberal Studies program include Georgetown University, St. John's College,

43

and the New School for Social Research.

Georgetown University

Georgetown University's Liberal Studies Program, leading to the degree of Master of Arts in Liberal Studies (M.A.L.S.), is a multidisciplinary thirty-credit master's program. The distribution of credits is: one three-credit "Core Course" (selected from a grouping of designated courses), completed within the first two semesters of study; one three-credit "Human Values" course; a three-credit "Integrating Seminar Project," and seven three-credit courses selected from any appropriate course offerings, including the Core courses and Human Values courses. In addition, students complete short "reflective essays" one-third of the way through the program and again two-thirds of the way through. The essays describe the student's courses and illuminate a particular theme, problem, or question.

In its publications, Georgetown University describes its Liberal Studies Program as resting on the belief

> that human life and human action have meaning and that human beings, throughout their lives, must seek it out and live by its implication. The course of study--which engages students in reading, reflection, and discussion--is meant to bring them the range of knowledge and vision to lead wise and rewarding lives.

In keeping with the Catholic tradition of Georgetown University, emphasis is placed not only on the intellectual disciplines but also on the search for and continual reassessment of personal values and convictions. The combination is intended to integrate students' studies with their daily lives, opinions, and activities and to continue to develop their minds beyond formal graduate-level education.

The Human Values courses are central to the philosophical and values orientation of Georgetown's program. The courses focus on values themes and are taught by philosophers, theologians, historians, and sociologists. An example of a Human Values course is "Values in Conflict," which examines a number of areas in current social life where values actually conflict. Taught by a philosopher, one of the key areas studied is family or generational conflict.

Students read works by Margaret Mead and Erik Erikson, as well as selections from Aristotle, Plato and Aquinas. They also view some classic films, including *Padre Padrone*, and discuss plays relevant to the theme, such as *Oedipus Rex* and *Hamlet*.

An additional example of a Human Values course is "Alienation and Self-Identity," taught by a theologian. The course describes the individual quest for self-identity, exploring the nature of the human self and its relation to society and contrasting the alienated individual with the revolutionary. Also discussed are the concepts of God and of the world as "alien other" as these are explored in the works of Sartre, Berger, Luckmann, Freud, and Joyce.

Human Values courses are similar to the Human Values Core courses in that they confront questions of value but do not necessarily cover as broad a subject matter. The course "A World in Process," for example, deals with contemporary scientific and philosophical visions of the world and with the myths, metaphors, and paradigms whereby we consider the question of human destiny. Readings are drawn from Alfred North Whitehead, Teilhard de Chardin, and others.

Specific Human Values Core courses are repeated once a year or every second year while Human Values courses change every semester. Thus, students have a wide choice of elective courses within the requirement of "Human Values."

St. John's College

St. John's College is unique among American institutions of higher learning in its adherence to an inclusive, wholly required undergraduate curriculum. Adopted in 1937, the four-year course of undergraduate study is based upon reading and discussion of original writings of the great minds of our civilization and reasserts the tradition of classical liberal education.

In 1966 St. John's College received a grant from the Carnegie Corporation to assist with the development and implementation of a Graduate Institute in Liberal Education at the Santa Fe, New Mexico campus, and classes began in the summer of 1967. In 1975, discussions for establishing the Graduate Institute in Annapolis, Maryland were begun and classes were offered beginning with the summer of 1977.

The Graduate Institute in Liberal Education at St. John's College offers a course of liberal studies leading to a

Master of Arts degree. Like the undergraduate program, it is based on the educational philosophy and teaching methods of St. John's College. The graduate program is offered for eight weeks in the summer in Santa Fe and in Annapolis and for sixteen weeks (Monday and Thursday evenings) during the academic year in Albuquerque and Santa Fe.

St. John's describes its Graduate Institute as "founded to provide mature, college-educated men and women with an opportunity to consider fundamental questions raised and developed within the traditions which have formed our civilization." At the heart of the approach to learning at St. John's is the selection of original texts chosen more for their originality of thought or power of reasoning than for any supposed completeness of coverage of subject matter.

The teaching and learning philosophy at St. John's is entirely interdisciplinary and it is an institutional assumption that departmental or disciplinary divisions are necessarily artificial. For the sake of convenience, however, the curriculum is divided into four regions of social, broadly poetic, scientific, and religious or philosophic studies, formally named "Politics and Society," "Literature," "Mathematics and Science," and "Philosophy and Theology." The unity--rather than the differences--of these broad divisions is stressed and students are encouraged to "cross-reference" their learning and classroom discussions.

Courses at St. John's are divided into three types: the seminar, the tutorial and the praeceptorial. The seminar, limited to about eighteen students, meets one evening each week and consists of discussions moderated by two tutors. The tutorial meets twice as often as the seminar and consists of a class of ten to fourteen students and one tutor. Assignments are shorter than in the seminar, and emphasis is placed upon close reading and criticism. Praeceptorials are classes of eight to twelve students and one tutor who study a single book or problem. The praeceptorials generally meet once a week for four hours. In the praeceptorial each student selects a topic pertinent to the book or problem under discussion and, with the help of a tutor, writes a long essay. The praeceptorial essays written over the course of three or four sessions replace the conventional master's thesis for Institute students.

All seminars and tutorials in a given segment of the curriculum study the same materials. The texts studied for the seminar in the "Politics and Society" segment, for example, include Plutarch, *Lives of Lycurgus and Solon*;

Plato, *Republic;* Aquinas, *Treatise on Law;* and Locke, *Second Treatise of Civil Government.* The tutorial for the same segment focuses on Aristotle, *Nicomachean Ethics;* Hobbes, *Leviathan;* the *U.S. Constitution;* and other related works. Praeceptorial topics include Aristotle, *Politics;* Rousseau, *The Social Contract;* Smith, *The Wealth of Nations;* and Tolstoy, *War and Peace.*

By limiting the basic mode of teaching to discussion rather than lecture, St. John's College is seeking to reaffirm its conviction that the ultimate authority in the most important matters is the intelligence in each student, and that this is best fostered in open discourse.

New School for Social Research

The New School for Social Research offers a thirty-credit Master of Arts in Liberal Studies (M.A.L.S.) through its Graduate Faculty. The program was originally divided into three tracts--Philosophy and the Arts, Psychology and Sociology, and Political Science and Economics--united by a series of seminars in the History of Ideas. As the program developed, the curriculum was altered to assure that students gained breadth as well as depth of knowledge. The present structure emphasizes individual program planning and each entering student meets with the program director and student advisor to discuss the goals he or she seeks to achieve in the degree program. A curriculum based on these articulated goals is then proposed, although it is subject to change as the student's plans become more clearly defined in the course of study. In addition to the thirty-six credits, students are required to complete a Master's Project to conclude the degree program.

The philosophy and ideas that provide the intellectual framework for the M.A.L.S. Program find their basis in the origins of the Graduate Faculty of the New School. Established in 1933 as the University in Exile, the Graduate Faculty was originally seen as a center for distinguished European scholars who fled totalitarian governments. A year after its founding, the University in Exile was converted to the Graduate Faculty of the New School, and the first degree programs, in political and social science, were offered. The emigre scholars on the Graduate Faculty in the early thirties defined many of the characteristics that continue today--a broad international outlook and an understanding that ideas, issues and subjects should be studied within the larger framework of our civilization. As a result of the origins of the Graduate Faculty at New School, the M.A.L.S. Program stresses liberal education as a form of liberation from prejudice, fear, and intellectual or ideological oppression. The accent on many courses offered by New School's M.A.L.S. Program therefore rests on the belief that freedom from political and intellectual coercion is the source of meaning in human life.

A course which reflects this broad and humanistic perspective is "The Spanish Civil War Fifty Years Later: History, Politics, Art," which was offered in the spring term of 1986 to coincide with the anniversary of the Spanish Civil War. The interdisciplinary course explores the role that the Spanish Civil War played in the political life of Europe and America in the thirties and focuses on the writers, artists, and composers who flocked to the loyalist cause in defense of democracy and socialism, or in the fight to defeat fascism. The course takes an unsentimental look at the art of the war and the relationship of that art to actual events. Both "high art" and "popular art," such as posters and magazine illustrations of both the Republicans and the Fascists, are utilized as examples of the way visual materials played a prominent role in the civil war. Readings include Hemingway's *For Whom The Bell Tolls* and *The Fifth Column* as well as selections from works by Dos Passos, Sinclair, Orwell, and Koestler. Three films complement the readings and discussions: Iven's *Spanish Earth,* Malraux's *La Sierra de Teruel,* and Bunel's *Pan y Tierra.*

Other courses consistent with the program's general theme include "Racism Within Modernity: Racial Domination and Liberation," which examines the socio-political and psychological conditions that gave rise to and sustained racism, using South Africa and the American South as key examples; a team-taught ethics course which examines some of the principal stances that men and women in Western history have taken regarding questions of right and wrong, good and evil; and "Social Theories of Fascism," which examines the history of social theory in the twentieth century with special emphasis on theoretical understanding of fascism.

Multidisciplinary Programs with Core Courses

One of the most enduring models for Graduate Liberal Studies programs is provided by institutions which require multidisciplinary core courses in the liberal arts followed by elective courses. Such programs tend to reinforce the interdisciplinary nature of Graduate Liberal Studies while avoiding an overly eclectic approach to learning. Examples of such curricular structures include Duke University, The Johns Hopkins University and Brooklyn College (CUNY).

Duke University

Duke University's Master of Arts in Liberal Studies Program, established in the fall of 1984, consists of thirty credits, or nine courses followed by a final project. At least three of the nine courses must be taken in specially designed interdisciplinary core courses.

The core courses in Duke's M.A.L.S. Program constitute the curricular basis of the program and share several fundamental characteristics. Each core course is designed to be a model of interdisciplinary learning and is organized around a topic general enough to demand treatment from a variety of perspectives. Each course relates concerns of established academic disciplines to crucial issues of life experience; each opens up essentially unlimited prospects for further inquiry and reflection. Core courses may contain components of the humanities, the social sciences and the sciences. Some of the core courses are taught jointly by faculty members from different disciplines, and several of the courses are intended to reflect Duke's strength in the natural sciences.

Core courses at Duke University include "The Nature of Being Human" and "Evolution: Formulation, Impact, and Controversies." The former is an exploration of the nature of being human from essentially literary and historical perspectives and surveys a broad range of primary sources from various periods while dealing with four characteristics which set humans apart from all other beings: the capacity to speak and, by extension, to make various uses and misuses of language spoken and written; the capacity to live histori-cally, i.e., trying to repossess and reassess the past; the notion of human destiny, both individual and collective, as focused particularly in the tradition of tragedy; and the need to understand our relationship to nature.

The core course on evolution explores the historical, philosophical, and scientific changes that led Darwin to his formulation of the theory of evolution, and scrutinizes its assumptions and flaws. The course also examines the impact of the theory of evolution on nineteenth-century biology and society in general. The roles that advances in genetics and biology have played in the development of a modern synthetic evolutionary theory and current controversies in evolutionary theory are emphasized.

Other core courses offered by Duke's M.A.L.S. Program include "War as a Social Institution," "Medicine and Literature," and "Literature, Art, and Social Vision Since the French Revolution." The core courses are altered each term to provide students with variety and with a freedom to select courses that are appropriate for their program of study.

The Johns Hopkins University

The Johns Hopkins University's Master of Liberal Arts Program was established in 1962 and is one of the oldest graduate liberal studies programs in the country. The thirty-credit master's degree was originally designed with a specific "History of Ideas" focus which emphasized the interdisciplinary approach to inquiry fostered by Hopkins faculty such as Arthur O. Lovejoy and George Boas. In recent years, the "History of Ideas" as a methodological approach for the M.L.A. Program has been replaced by a broader understanding of the term. The "History of Ideas" has thus become the rubric for special interdisciplinary core courses created exclusively for and open only to students enrolled in the M.L.A. Program. These courses are designed to expose students to areas of intellectual inquiry from a broad perspective which links together concepts, ideas and genres from different disciplines. The History of Ideas courses, while often dealing with works, ideas, and terms associated with a highly specialized graduate-level seminar, do not assume a specific undergraduate major in any one academic discipline. Even in instances in which History of Ideas seminar students have similar academic backgrounds, for example in the humanities, the course emphasizes linkage with other disciplines rather than a narrow or highly specialized approach.

A typical History of Ideas seminar is "Oedipus: Myth,

Folktale, Drama, Complex," which begins with a survey of the ancient sources for the myth of Oedipus and continues with an examination of Sophocles' drama, *Oedipus the King,* as one variant among several that were known to the ancient Greeks. Students also study a collection of medieval and modern folktales which are related or similar in origin. The second half of the seminar focuses on modern interpretations of the Oedipus myth, dramatic and psychoanalytic, and includes readings of modern Oedipus dramas by Gide and Cocteau as well as Freud's major statements on the Oedipus Complex.

Another History of Ideas seminar is "Technology and Culture, 1919-1939," which examines the interrelationship between technological development and the arts--particularly painting and sculpture, architecture, film, and literature--in the period between the two world wars. Topics range from the image of the modern city in the arts during that period to the idea of progress, especially technologically-based progress as it is manifested in events such as the New York World's Fair of 1939.

Both courses present material within a broad historical and intellectual context, and in papers students are encouraged to explore the ideas in the courses from a variety of viewpoints and without particular reference to the methodologies of specific academic disciplines. In addition to the History of Ideas Seminars, students also enroll in three liberal arts elective courses and complete a three-credit master's project. Upon faculty approval students may also complete a formal master's thesis for six credits.

Brooklyn College (City University of New York)

Brooklyn College's Special Baccalaureate Program, begun in the mid-1950's, has a well-established reputation in the area of the liberal arts for non-traditional students. In 1980, Brooklyn College extended its commitment to the part-time student with the inauguration of its Master of Arts in Liberal Studies (M.A.L.S.) Program. The curriculum is interdisciplinary and includes courses in communications, the humanities, social sciences and natural and computer sciences.

At the heart of the program are two six-credit core seminars which cover perspectives from religion, philosophy, psychology, comparative literature, art and television/film in the first seminar and archeology/anthropology, history, sociology, physics/chemistry, computer information science, and biology in the second seminar. The first seminar introduces the treatment of the human ideal by the major religions, and the last portion of the second seminar introduces the notion of human intervention in effecting the idea of a particular culture. The course is cumulative in its approach with each unit (usually two class sessions) building upon the preceding unit and anticipating questions to be raised by succeeding units regarding the development of human values in particular cultures and particular times. The course is team-taught, and each unit is presented by a different instructor who has participated in discussions during the previous unit and who will participate in the succeeding unit to provide continuity.

Graduate Liberal Studies Programs with Major Areas of Concentration

Although Graduate Liberal Studies programs are overwhelmingly interdisciplinary in their approach to liberal learning, some universities have found that a major area of concentration lends focus to the degree. When a Graduate Liberal Studies program offers or requires a concentration in a specific area, however, it is generally within a broader context than is the case with a disciplinary master's degree. Frequently such programs offer concentrations in a particular interdisciplinary area such as literature and art, or the History of Science. Examples of schools with areas of concentration for their Graduate Liberal Studies programs include Wesleyan University and Harvard University.

Wesleyan University

The Graduate Liberal Studies program at Wesleyan, leading to the Master of Arts in Liberal Studies (M.A.L.S.), was established in 1952, and it is the first program of its type in the country. The curriculum of Wesleyan's program is designed to provide a range of choices to both degree and non-degree students. The core of the program is its interdisciplinary Liberal Studies courses, which challenge the student to cut through arbitrary boundaries to comprehend the inventiveness of the human mind in finding and imposing order upon the course of human experience through time.

52

Core Liberal Studies courses include "Three Classical Heroes," which explores the classical Greek concept of the ideal of excellence as embodied in the hero; "Political Economy in the Age of Keynes," which traces and compares the historical development of large-scale political and economic organization in the U.S. and Germany between 1870 and 1945; and "The Nightingale and the Cuckoo: Opera as Literature and Myth," which is an examination of the literary, dramatic, and mythic aspects of opera as an art form.

In addition to the Liberal Studies core courses, the program at Wesleyan also requires a concentration in one of the traditional fields--arts, humanities, mathematics, science, social studies--or in special, self-designed fields. There are no specific required courses in the area of concentration, but each area requires a minimum of two Critical Perspective courses and, depending on the area selected, six or seven additional courses. Critical Perspective courses are those courses which provide a foundation in a discipline, are "keystones" within a field of study, or deal with critical methodologies or techniques. In addition to the courses in the area of concentration, students must also enroll in two courses outside the area of concentration.

Harvard University

Harvard University's Master of Liberal Arts Program consists of forty graduate credits of which twenty-eight must be in one of eighteen fields of concentration such as anthropology and archaeology, biology, dramatic arts, English and American literature, fine arts, government, history, psychology, religion, sociology and women's studies. Within the major field of study at least twenty of the required twenty-eight credits are in regular upper-level courses; the remaining eight credits are fulfilled by a four-credit seminar in the major field and a four-credit independent research course with a teaching member of the Harvard Faculty of Arts and Sciences. The remaining twelve credits are fulfilled through a four-credit seminar outside the major field of study and an additional eight credits outside the broad area in which the major field of study falls. For example, if a student selects "government" as a major field, which falls under "social sciences," he or she must complete eight credits in the humanities or natural sciences.

Modes of Delivery

Graduate Liberal Studies programs are generally identified with part-time students who are attending courses in the evening, since this model is the most common. There are, however, well-established Graduate Liberal Studies programs which derive much of their identity and often their curricular structure from a different format such as courses offered primarily for students attending full-time during a summer session, courses offered exclusively on weekends, and programs which combine courses offered at the institution with independent study for a non-resident population. Examples of such programs include Dartmouth College, College of Notre Dame of Maryland and the University of Oklahoma.

Dartmouth College

The Master of Arts in Liberal Studies Program at Dartmouth College is designed for individuals who want to engage in both directed and independent work on subjects that are not bound by the curricula of traditional disciplines. Students have the opportunity to work with faculty to design an individual interdisciplinary plan of study based on personal or professional aims.

Dartmouth's program is primarily a summer program although students may also enroll in the fall, winter or spring terms. Requirements for the degree include a minimum of three terms in residence--three ten-week summer terms or two ten-week summer terms and a fall, winter, or spring term. Thus it is possible for an individual not living in the vicinity of Dartmouth to enroll in courses for three summer terms to complete the M.A.L.S. degree, and, in fact, students from all over the United States have completed their degree by attending only during the summers at Dartmouth. Housing in dormitories can be arranged, or students may arrange their own lodgings while pursuing their studies at Dartmouth. The program enrolls approximately one hundred students during the summer, about half of whom reside in the dormitories, and about thirty students during the fall, winter, and spring terms. The advantages of a resident summer program include providing the students with a sense of intellectual community and letting them focus on their studies without competition from a job or other commitments. The disadvantage is that such a summer program will likely be limited to people who are not employed or teachers who have summers free.

College of Notre Dame of Maryland

The College of Notre Dame of Maryland is a small liberal arts women's college in Baltimore, Maryland and since 1975 has developed a weekend college format for its continuing education programs. The college established a coeducational, part-time, thirty-three credit Graduate Liberal Studies program in 1986 which offers courses exclusively on Saturdays. Courses on Saturdays are offered from 8:30 a.m. until 11:15 a.m., 12:00 noon until 2:45 p.m and 3:00 p.m. until 5:45 p.m. Although many students enroll in two classes, only in exceptional cases are students permitted to enroll in three courses at a time.

Classes offered include "Literature of the Examined Life," which explores selected works of literature representative of man's passion for knowledge and for life; "The Free Speech Tradition in America," which studies the historical and philosophical traditions of free speech in American society and of the free speech doctrine as set forth in the Constitution; and "The City as Art," which views cities from ancient time to contemporary centers of life emphasizing architecture, city patterns, and planned environments and habitats.

University of Oklahoma

The University of Oklahoma has developed a successful Master of Liberal Studies Program, which combines resident study during the summer at the University with directed, independent study during the fall and spring terms. The course of study is segmented into an initial two-week Introductory Seminar followed by a period, usually one year, of Directed Study. The independent Directed Study is pursued at the student's own pace with communication maintained through mail, telephone, or personal visits with faculty advisors. This portion of the program is followed by a three-week Colloquium during which advisement for the thesis begins. Advanced Directed Study and work on the thesis also proceeds at the student's own pace. The program is concluded by a two-week Advanced Seminar providing additional interactive experience with other students and faculty and a time for the student's thesis defense.

The University of Oklahoma's format allows students from diverse geographical areas to complete a master's degree while maintaining full-time employment since the summer courses are relatively short and can encompass vacation time. The program carefully coordinates the intensive residential experience during the summer with the independent Directed Study during the remainder of the year.

Conclusion

The diversity of Graduate Liberal Studies programs indicates the wide range of possibilities open to institutions of higher learning interested in promoting liberal arts education at the graduate level for part-time and non-traditional students. This diversity further points to the fact that each institution must develop a program that addresses its own strengths, acknowledges its limitations and is in accordance with its overall mission and institutional identity. Those colleges and universities with successful programs--in terms of both numbers of students and academic quality--are precisely those schools which have well-articulated objectives in the area of continuing education and in liberal learning and which recognize that structured learning does not end with full-time study or at age twenty-five. Although these successful programs may serve as models for other institutions, they can never be regarded as wholly adaptable to other geographic locations, student populations, institutional contexts or ideological frameworks. The ability to coordinate well-articulated objectives and place them within the context of what can be accomplished well--whether it consists of a weekend format, a summer residential program, or a highly structured curriculum--may ultimately be a school's single most significant determining factor in establishing and successfully maintaining a Graduate Liberal Studies program of high quality.

David B. House, Ph.D.
The Johns Hopkins University

THE INTERDISCIPLINARY HEART OF LIBERAL STUDIES

Overview

The educational center of most Graduate Liberal Studies curricula seems clearly to be the interdisciplinary course. This fact derives from the explicit goal of Graduate Liberal Studies programs to provide a foundation for significant integration of disciplines in discovering knowledge of the "worlds" in which we live, and in comprehending how diverse academic disciplines broaden and deepen our grasp of the seminal ideas of our civilization and of the critical problems of life and the mind that inform the cultures of the past and the present.

Every perspective constitutes a limited illumination of the meaning of the conditions of our experience and of its historical grounding. Each discipline contributes its unique and vital insights and imposes its own limitations. Interdisciplinary study encourages our intellects and sensibilities to cut through arbitrary boundaries and to explore the values and contributions of diverse modes of seeking and comprehending knowledge.

Such courses create a disciplined and systematic confrontation with the inventiveness of the human mind in finding or imposing order upon our experience. The interdisciplinary course is the essential educational structure by which we insure an active flow of fundamental ideas that illuminate the total range of our experience. By its means, we seek to combat the entropy of what Whitehead termed "inert" knowledge.

Core courses in Graduate Liberal Studies programs are, without exception, interdisciplinary in organization and focus. Aside from the general justifications for core programs, there is the expectation that core interdisciplinary courses will aid in filling those unavoidable gaps with which even the best undergraduate education burdens us. Moreover, interdisciplinary courses have the unique function of reminding us that liberal learning literally frees the mind and sensibility from the constraints that are often the legacy of an over-specialized, narrowly focused undergraduate career.

Core studies must also be viewed in the context of the particular kind of student who is attracted to Graduate Liberal Studies programs, i.e., principally adults who are re-entering the educational process after absences of varying lengths of time. Adults often experience this re-entry process with a considerable degree of anxiety about their competence to take up once again the rigors and discipline of serious academic study. In this regard, core studies serve the dual purpose of reintroducing the student to the task of interdisciplinary study (the search for a significant synthesis of knowledge) and providing a common basis for exploration of some fundamental and perennial questions and ideas that have shaped the human past and persist in the present.

Since most Graduate Liberal Studies programs require some form of culminating project in the form of an essay, thesis, comprehensive exam, or project, training early on in the skills and values of interdisciplinary inquiry is considered crucial. Most culminating projects in Graduate Liberal Studies programs are designed in such a way that the students are given the opportunity to exhibit the fruits of their growth in interdisciplinary inquiry in a substantive, articulated manner. The final project, be it essay, creative work, or comprehensive exam, provides the students with the intellectual challenge of bringing their academic program to a significant culmination by using those insights, methods, and perspectives, the corpus of liberal learning, to articulate, independently, a study that is both correlative and integrative.

Defining the Interdisciplinary Courses

Interdisciplinary courses are exotic hybrids in the world of education. While their parent stock, the traditional disciplines, are beyond reproach, interdisciplinary courses have been subject to intense suspicion. The 1980 Rockefeller Commission on the Humanities provides an excellent case in point. It strongly recommended "integrative courses" for the undergraduate curriculum but with the caveat that the appellation "interdisciplinary" can "disguise shoddy, ill-conceived courses that merely dilute a variety of subjects rather than unite them in a coherent and imaginative synthesis." So, the typical debate is opened with the Commission laying before us a spectrum of options running from "dilution" to "coherent and imaginative synthesis." Metaphors such as "dilution" and "watered down" as substitutes for serious analysis abound in every academic discussion of the academic viability of interdisciplinary courses.

Following the implications of the metaphor "watered down" to its logical conclusion, we discover that disciplinary courses, by contrast, are the distillation of knowledge, the concentrated essence. Just as there is dishonesty in the bartender who "waters down" his spirits, there is also the suspicion that the professor who strays from the essence of a discipline is engaged in a form of intellectual dishonesty. Suppose, however, for the sake of argument, I am a gardener. Then the metaphor takes on a radically different and powerful connotation. To "water down" my plants means to supply them with the essential ingredient for their continuing health and growth. Let us explore the thesis that the watering down of disciplinary knowledge by interdisciplinary inquiry is precisely providing that critical nourishment that disciplines require if they are not to wither and die, i.e., become "inert" knowledge.

The term "discipline" is generally taken to refer to a branch of learning or knowledge. The Latin prefix *inter* means between or among, but many words have been constructed with this prefix which are interesting, active verbs. Thus, while *inter* seems to designate a place, most often it designates a process, e.g., interpose, intercede, interdict, intervene, and interact. Interdisciplinary is one of these new words, and if we assume for the moment that knowledge is essentially organized into disciplines, to talk of some body of knowledge "between" disciplines seems odd indeed. However, if there is a body of knowledge that falls outside disciplinary boundaries, the form of inquiry which brings that knowledge into view needs to be looked at very closely. In what follows, we shall follow the clue that the "inter" in interdisciplinary refers to an active process, a process of thinking.

We generally presume that a discipline has in view some particular subject matter, that the phenomena it studies are limited in scope, though it may encompass a rather large portion of our known world. Another way of putting this is that a discipline gets its definition in part by what it declines to study. In order to proceed with its task of acquiring and organizing knowledge of its subject matter, a discipline develops and employs various analytical and investigative tools which we call methodologies. These both guide and limit the scope of disciplinary inquiry and provide implicit criteria for what counts as knowledge within a field of study.

In general, the power of disciplinary thought to illuminate (in depth) its subject matter derives from the limiting of the focus of methodological inquiry to a finite set of phenomena. An analogy may illustrate this: disciplinary thought is like a very intense searchlight, narrowly focused on a limited field--the end in view being the clearest, most precise, and most intense illumination that is possible.

One of the most interesting characteristics of the systematic attempt to extend disciplinary knowledge is that the more one tries to make a rigorous, self-contained science (a body of systematized knowledge) of one's discipline, the more strikingly does it begin to slip away, or as Hegel might put it, "slide over into its opposite(s)."

It should not surprise us, therefore, to find that it is at the boundaries, the limits, of a discipline's field of study that we find the greatest paradoxes and antinomies. For example, the law of supply and demand appears to be a reasonably powerful descriptive explanation for the operation of some economic systems, yet consider how little it really explains if we leave out of account the behavior and psychology of people. Some economists, perhaps Adam Smith and Karl Marx, have been bold enough to suggest that economic principles *are* sufficient to explain human behavior and psychology. Such enterprises reveal what appears to be the great temptation of disciplinary thinking--intellectual imperialism.

What is unusual about an interdisciplinary course is not its subject matter but the mode of thinking that takes place in it. In short, when people teach or learn in an interdisciplinary course, they engage in a style of thinking that is quite distinct from what typically occurs in disciplinary thought or inquiry.

Interdisciplinary thinking is the shuttle or movement of thought between two or more disciplinary perspectives. This movement of thought does not mean merely the juxtaposition of two perspectives--placing their knowledge before us as two distinct views of the "same" thing. Of course, multi-disciplinary courses can be created by the successive juxtaposition of several disciplines which seek to comprehend the "same" thing. But when no attempt is made to make a coherent and imaginative synthesis, you do not have a genuine interdisciplinary course. Interdisciplinary thinking is a kind of thinking whereby the incompleteness and limits of each disciplinary view are partially corrected by the other, with the result that a new and broader vision is brought before the mind. Such thinking, therefore, clearly involves a transcendence of the boundaries of the disciplines *and*, more importantly, of the kind of thinking that occurs within those boundaries.

As suggested earlier, disciplinary thinking achieves its explanatory power by the precision of its conceptual constructs (by their clarity and distinctness, to use Descartes' phrase) and by declining to use those constructs to explain everything. The ideal of disciplinary thinking is to press those constructs to their explanatory limit and to bring all phenomena in the fold under their sway. Interdisciplinary thought, as a form of the thinking transcendence of disciplinary limits, proceeds by stepping outside the limits of the organized body of knowledge to assess what it has achieved and to judge to what extent its (the discipline's) achievements fall short of its actual intent. In this respect, interdisciplinary thinking permits us to learn what we can say about a thought position that cannot be said within it. It is a sort of higher order commentary on the adequacy of a thought position already achieved, organized, and systematized.

What this critical appraisal of the disciplines' conceptual schema or methodologies reveals, of course, varies greatly. It might show the necessity for new, complementary, saving constructs. Sometimes the criticism brings into view altogether new principles of comprehension--principles not formally entailed at the lower level. The discovery of new principles in some instances becomes then the architectural floor for a new story in the house of knowledge.

I use this last metaphor, the "house of knowledge," intentionally. It is a common assumption of disciplinary thought that the various disciplines of knowledge provide the foundations for any higher stories that are built as our knowledge expands, and, moreover, that the upper stories of the "house" must be confined *well within* the supporting base. What interdisciplinary thinking reveals, on the contrary, is that more concepts, more "objects," are needed than those provided in the supporting base.

Let me express this thesis in a slightly different way. One principal result of Nietzsche's thinking was to deny *any* absolute knowledge and to posit only a perspectival knowing. "There is only a perspective seeing, only a perspective knowing, and the more affects we allow to speak about one thing, the more eyes, different eyes, we can use to observe one thing, the more complete will our concept of this thing be . . ." Nietzsche's point is that any perspective (read discipline), by the very fact of being single and definable against all others, excludes in significant ways elements of other perspectives. Interdisciplinary thinking is a form of thought whereby we rise to ever wider perspectives--overcoming the arbitrary isolation of entities understood only in their disciplinary settings and bringing us to a more comprehensive vision of the world of phenomena. Every body of disciplinary knowledge is a foreground knowledge, an arbitrary stopping point. What it conceals is its deep background. Interdisciplinary inquiry by its deepening analyses of the foreground can show the hidden background more intensely and wisely.

A Model of an Interdisciplinary Course

There is a multitude of excellently designed and thoughtfully developed interdisciplinary courses in Graduate Liberal Studies programs across the nation. I have selected one model to look at with a view to seeing how the instructional purpose of the course is embedded in its organization, its pedagogy, and its variety of focus. In looking at this model, perhaps we can get some sense of how interdisciplinary courses "work."

Let us look at an interdisciplinary course designed at Dartmouth College by three professors from the disciplines of physics, art, and philosophy. The course description is as follows:

OPTICS, ART, PHILOSOPHY: APPEARANCE AND REALITY. Three instructors from three different fields and departments will together discuss problems relating to the nature of physical reality, the mechanisms of our visual perception of this reality, the role of art in bridging the gap between our perceptions and what is felt emotionally, and the philosophical questions concerning the nature of art, of knowledge, of reality itself.

The first week of the course is devoted to an examination of what we know about the physical nature of light, particularly about the sensations of pure spectral light and the colors created by various mixtures of light. The second week focuses upon epistemological problems that grow immediately out of human perception and the common-sense view of

62

physical reality. The third and fourth weeks are devoted to the ways that colors interact with each other so as often to systematically deceive us. Students participate in laboratory exercises designed to develop sensitivity to color relations. The artistic motivations and theories that inform these exercises are compared to physiological and psychological theories of perception based upon identified mechanisms of eye and brain.

The final three weeks begin with discussions of different theories of imaging: the eye, the camera, holograms, and television. The geometrical theory of perspective and its relation to physical imaging is contrasted to the objectives and accomplishments of Renaissance artists in the development of linear perspective. These discussions are followed by slide presentations which examine a variety of artistic points of view. Impressionism is considered from the perspective of its use of light and atmosphere to depict nature; surrealism is looked at as a means of moving away from the outer world to an inner world of dreams and the unconscious; expressionism is considered in terms of its explorations of automatism and gesture.

The course concludes by confronting fundamental questions in the field of aesthetics, such as: what is a work of art? what is the nature of aesthetic experience?

From just this brief description of this very rich course, it should be clear that the question of the distinction between appearance and reality is interpreted very differently when viewed from the perspectives of the disciplines of physics, art, and philosophy. What is noteworthy in the description of the course is that all three professors would be discussing the ideas and issues that the course focuses upon. The intent clearly seems to be to explore how disciplinary perspectives require broader vistas and complementary fields of knowledge if synthesis of any significant nature is to occur. Moreover, the assumption seems to be that our knowledge of the relationship between perception and the kind of distinctions made between appearance and reality is most complete and coherent when such integrative inquiries have been undertaken.

This course is an excellent paradigm for interdisciplinary thinking because its ultimate purpose is to find important ways in which different forms of knowing, from empirical observation to conceptual analysis, are all required in order to gain a synthetic perspective. The indispensability of fields of knowledge for each other and for gaining wider and more comprehensive vision is not only demonstrated in the interplay between the disciplines but it is experienced directly by the students as they attempt to understand and provide linkages between very diverse fields of knowledge. To discover that one must have some significant comprehension of the physical properties of light if one is to understand and deal competently with essentially contestable questions in the field of aesthetics is to transcend knowingly the arbitrary boundaries of disciplinary knowledge and, thereby, to attain synthetic understanding.

Allie Frazier, Ph.D
Hollins College

BEYOND EXPERTISE: GRADUATE LIBERAL STUDIES PROGRAMS AND THE PRACTICE OF TEACHING

Imagine an age of ruin, asks Alasdair MacIntyre, an age in which all that remain of the natural sciences are fragments of knowledge shorn of theoretical contexts, instruments whose use has been forgotten, and terms bandied about but no longer rooted in processes of inquiry which lend them meaning. What is worse, imagine nobody realizing that what passes for science does not deserve the name. A "disquieting suggestion," indeed (1-2). Yet MacIntyre evokes this apocalyptic spectre only to make the more disquieting contention that in truth the world of morality is in just such disarray. We possess merely the "simulacra" of a lost theory and practice of morality (2-50).

Like Plato's critique of the shadow world of the Cave, MacIntyre's parable is more than disquieting: it calls into question an habitual certitude about the worth and efficacy of our deepest involvements. Part of its power lies in our ability to apply it to other contexts. Disquieting suggestion #1 about science leads to disquieting suggestion #2 about morality which leads to disquieting suggestion #3 about X. So, then, one further disquieting suggestion--what if the practice of teaching has come to such a pass? Imagine ourselves left with only the motions and movements of that authentic practice devoid of connection with real intellectual transformation, gears spinning furiously but never meshing.

Surely we have heard this last suggestion before. MacIntyres aplenty inhabit the sundry commissions of higher education; their pronouncements emblazon the pages of the *Chronicle of Higher Education.* I hasten to disassociate myself from these Jeremiahs. The power of MacIntyre's parable lies not in any parallels which we can discern between his imagined world of dissolution and the actual practice of teaching but in its ability to force a reexamination of what constitutes authentic teaching and a search for its contemporary exemplars. The parable gives pause--not truth. Each of us, confronted with an apocalyptic vision of the dissolution of the genuine practice of teaching, must say

"No, wait! Look here and here and there. In these pockets within our colleges and universities the authentic practice of teaching is reborn again and again." In this chapter I wish to do just this by showing how Graduate Liberal Studies programs provide contexts where the practice of teaching is rejuvenated.[1]

Before we take leave of Alasdair MacIntyre, let me borrow his concept of a "practice" to guide our discussion of the practice of teaching.

> By a "practice" I am going to mean any coherent and complex form of socially cooperative human activity through which goods internal to that form of activity are realized in the course of trying to achieve those standards of excellence which are appropriate to, and partially definitive of, that form of activity, with the result that human powers to achieve excellence, and human conceptions of the ends and goods involved are systematically extended (175).

If we assume MacIntyre's definition of a practice, then Graduate Liberal Studies programs, as pockets of excellence. would necessarily have to:

a) exhibit standards of excellence appropriate to teaching
b) enhance a faculty's powers to achieve excellence, and
c) expand our understanding of the goods internal to the practice of teaching.

In ordinary circumstances this would be a lot to ask of any academic program. It would seem especially a lot to ask of Graduate Liberal Studies programs, for these are programs offering Master's degrees which are not centered upon education for a profession. We speak, therefore, of programs

[1]I wish to thank two of my colleagues in DePaul's Master of Arts in Liberal Studies program, Drs. John Price and Arthur Thurner, both of whom exemplify what I argue here, for their helpful comments on an earlier version of this chapter.

which are stepchildren in the modern university. If it seems strange that the stepchild should exemplify the practice of teaching, then so be it. By restoring an independent purpose to the very label Master of Arts, Graduate Liberal Studies programs simultaneously enhance the practice of teaching in many sectors of the university.

A. Teaching And Context: Building A Program, Developing A Faculty

If the claims that I am making for Graduate Liberal Studies programs stemmed only from those who, as directors of such programs, feel called to spread the gospel, they would be subject to a substantial discount. In my experience, however, the faculty involved in the program make the strongest claims. What has surprised me is the number of faculty in our program at DePaul University who point to the period before the program enrolled a single student as a period which had an enormous impact upon their practice as teachers. Without ever consciously intending it, the faculty who created our Graduate Liberal Studies program simultaneously shaped themselves into a community of scholars intensely committed to the ideals of interdisciplinary learning.

The process was not quite as noble as it sounds. The faculty originally selected to plan the program were good teachers. All were solidly rooted in a discipline and possessed the capacity to stretch themselves beyond the safe confines of their area of expertise. Interdisciplinary teaching collapses when the teachers having practiced no discipline are unable to hold in tension rival traditions of learning. Yet schooled as we were in these diverse traditions, we found it hard to think programmatically. After all, the various disciplinary paradigms which we had absorbed provided the contexts in which the teaching that we do goes on. Disciplinary teaching gets carried on as a form of private enterprise--each teacher responsible for a particular segment of a larger operation--guided by the logic, the invisible hand, of the discipline. We found it hard to think programmatically because we rarely have to.

To design a Graduate Liberal Studies program is to create a context for learning that transcends a given disciplinary paradigm. What should that context be? How can it embody the strengths of scholarship, yet respond to the distinct purposes of adult learners? What are the appropriate standards for program coherence and excellence governing an interdisciplinary context? Even to address these questions, we had to forge a common language beyond the jargon, what Phillip Wheelwright calls the "steno-language," of our disciplinary endeavors. Yet that common tongue could not be some Esperanto, purged of the resonances of alternative modes of inquiry, interpretation, and judgment.

Clearly any academic program is more than a set of procedures or a packet of interesting courses. The presence of core courses in virtually all Graduate Liberal Studies programs points to a deeper level of coherence. What I have called the context of teaching is a large and only partially articulated cluster of assumptions about goals and outcomes, about the place of learning in human life, and about the knowledge most worth having as well as what it means to "have" knowledge. By having to articulate rather than assume such a context, teachers who plan Graduate Liberal Studies programs become clearer about the overall purposes of teaching. Rarely, if ever, beyond the department level do we have to ask ourselves how all the pieces fit together and in what frame. The exercise of creating a Graduate Liberal Studies program is a tutorial in the relativity of all our intellectual frameworks.

Our inability to afford team teaching in each of our core courses led us at DePaul to an innovation in curricular design which extended the benefits of planning the program. For six months three member teams worked to design each core course. Each member now teaches the course in rotation. Periodically the team meets to evaluate and revise the course. A new faculty member, slated to teach a core course, first sits in on team discussions and the course itself.

These procedures repeated the process of creating the program but at a much more specific level of interaction. In these frequently intense discussions we absorbed the meaning of the term interdisciplinary teaching. Gradually each team member began to lose both a possessive attitude towards the course and a defensiveness regarding its emergent shape. Instead, the shared sense of the course gradually gathering shape was incredibly invigorating. Periodic team meetings continue to be occasions for mutual instruction. Collegiality built into the very structure of the program has become the primary instrument for the individual's development as a teacher.

B. No Clones: Adult Learners And
The Practice Of Teaching

At a recent Graduate Liberal Studies colloquium at DePaul, Bernice Neugarten, Northwestern University's noted professor of adult psychology, tackled a number of myths about educating adults. Among the fashionable commonplaces which she questioned was the concept of adult stages of development. In fact, she argued, aging differentiates persons. Because adults diverge from the common denominator more rather than less the older they get, we cannot describe a predictable schedule of life transitions. The sheer diversity of educational programs which attract adult learners underscores Neugarten's perception. But what are its implications for teaching adults?

Contrary to pedagogical theories which place adults on a certain plateau in a schema of cognitive development, Neugarten's theory implicitly rejects the notion that adult learners are members of a different and higher caste and that, as such, each adult shares a set of goals and abilities. If this were the case, the practice of teaching Graduate Liberal Studies students would have no analogous effects on other areas of instruction. Adulthood, indeed, would seem to represent not the entelechy of the species but its transformation. A more appropriate metaphor to suggest the interconnectedness of all stages of the learning process might be Bernard Lonergan's image of an ongoing spiral of intellectual transformation in which the moments of experience, understanding, judgment and decision, comprising the learning cycle, occur again and again (273-76, 329-32, 612-16 and passim). The truism that adult learning must rest upon the touchstone of experience can then be reinterpreted in light of Lonergan's image of this intellectual spiral. The teacher of adults simply catalyzes a spiraling process which has become deeper, richer, and more compounded. This can only happen when students, at any level, come to recognize the process at work within themselves and, by articulating its procedures and products, push themselves further.

In contrast to programs developed to train professionals or to qualify the student for doctoral studies, Graduate Liberal Studies programs, as other essays in this volume stress, are designed to meet the diverse and divergent goals of our students. Personal and career goals freely mix. The desire to enter a community of thoughtfully engaged adults fuses with that of pursuing a cherished individual project. John Dewey's aphorism, "the fundamental purpose of education is to put people in possession of their powers," describes the intended outcome, common yet individualized, for all of our liberal studies students. To take this aphorism seriously is to become aware of how strange, how inappropriate the process of intellectual cloning really is. Even the role of the Socratic liberator in Plato's Myth of the Cave, which for many of us symbolizes an engaged and student-centered mode of teaching, apparently presumes a single path to knowledge and a single sun at the apex of intellectual achievement. To put students in possession of their distinctive powers, however, is to encourage students along paths that I will never take, to set them on their own path through a dark labyrinth towards truth which, viewed from distinct angles, must always appear novel.

The very inappropriateness of cloning operations within Graduate Liberal Studies programs raises fundamental questions about the good intended by other sorts of programs. The equation of rationality with routine activity characteristic of professional training appears suspect. Casting wave after wave of scholars upon the beachheads of ignorance fails to express the deepest intentions of our discipline-based doctoral programs. Perhaps we should revive an older notion of apprenticeship.

Dewey's aphorism, I hasten to add, does not imply that only the Socratic method, duly modified, works with Graduate Liberal Studies students. Accomplished scholars, practicing their disciplinary crafts, have an important role to play. I have found that they work best with our students not when they are introducing the rudimentary skills of their disciplines but when they move from comfortable plateaus towards the cliff-edge of thought where the scope and integrating power of their disciplinary perspectives are tested. In such classes scholars and students share a common intellectual risk, although at different levels of acumen. So, a noted biblical scholar teaches a course in our program which focuses not only on ancient parables but on the writings of modern practitioners of the genre like Kafka and Borges as well. By asking how all these versions work and acquire their peculiar power over the human imagination, he raises fundamental questions about the role and limits of narratives, sacred and secular, in shaping and reshaping human lives.

Despite their differences, Graduate Liberal Studies students do confront their teachers with certain common problems particularly at the initial stages of their programs. A person who enters a Graduate Liberal Studies program frequently combines the kind of courage and vulnerability of someone who steps outside of an accustomed groove, an expert practice, to attempt something new. The anxiety which naturally accompanies these traits is compounded by the length of time the person has been out of school. Students often do not recognize that the learning processes which occur outside of the school context are analogues to formal education. They worry excessively about rusty writing skills without realizing that each level of education requires new training in these skills. A healthy aversion to rote learning coupled with concerns about testing procedures also characterizes these students. Each of these problems typifies the transition from informal to formal learning contexts. The key to their resolution lies with a faculty committed to the core courses and conscious of the multiple purposes, practical and psychological as well as academic, which these courses must serve.

C. The Death of Expertise: Teaching The Core

Core courses are the marrow of any Graduate Liberal Studies program. They represent a dual challenge to any teacher. Interdisciplinary in character, they force us to become students again, to forsake the safe confines of expertise, and to explore a new and uncertain terrain. Customarily, as the initial courses in the student's program, they require a sensitive and structured approach to the common problems of adult students reentering the classroom. Each of these challenges deserves consideration.

To teach an interdisciplinary course demands the cultivation of a special form of "learned ignorance." A colleague who is deeply involved in graduate education for adults recently told me, "I try never to ask a question in a classroom discussion or seminar to which I know the answer." Stunned, I think, was my reaction to his comment. I am not sure that I agree with it fully. I think I know something about any question that I ask but it is usually not what could be called an answer. In any case the comment made me aware of how important the sense of mastery and control is to a teacher, even to one espousing the Socratic method. What, after all, were those long years of graduate training for if not to establish a base of knowledge through which answers to questions may be found and to grasp the mechanisms for building upon that base? If we take a different tack, don't we risk validating the suspicions of colleagues who view interdisciplinary seminars as the artful pooling of ignorance?

Such concerns have led many to suggest that interdisciplinary courses must be team taught. This seems to me to be begging the question. I have seen team-taught courses which should properly be labeled *dual-disciplinary.* Both instructors confined themselves to the familiar, to the trodden field of their respective areas of expertise. The students were given two mini-courses on a common theme or historical period. The work of integration was left to the students to manage as best they might. In a genuinely interdisciplinary course, even in the case where course materials are tightly restricted to the instructors' fields of knowledge, both teachers and students transgress disciplinary boundaries and move in a dialectical fashion to a new standpoint. So, team teaching, despite its obvious benefits, does not resolve the quandary which confronts one or more teachers hoping to engage students in interdisciplinary learning.

It goes without saying that persons who would be suitable choices for teaching the core courses must have a broad background of learning. They ought to exemplify an approach to scholarship which resists the drive to "know more and more about less and less." No one is a Renaissance person any longer, we are told. Yet many of our Graduate Liberal Studies faculty embody fragments of that ideal. Where narrow specialization breeds faculty unable to talk with one another, these individuals with their fragmentary realizations of integrated learning complement one another. The Graduate Liberal Studies program provides a context for their conversation. Again, this does not resolve our quandary. How many of these Renaissance fragments make a whole? Could we fit them all in the same classroom?

Inevitably, an individual or a team will confront an alien body of knowledge in a course that has not been deliberately sanitized. What do I do in DePaul's first core course, "Visions of the Self," with the models of selfhood exhibited in classic Hindu texts or drawn from the culture of Japanese Buddhism? How should I approach *King Lear* when I lack expert knowledge of its Elizabethan context or the history of its critical reception? Do I trade upon the students' sense of analogies with their own experience? Do I "stripmine" the text, as one scholar puts it, for its values, its nuggets of wisdom, neglecting if not ruining its own topography?

Discussions of analogous feelings, values, and conflicting world views certainly are appropriate in a core course. *In isolation,* however, these activities do come perilously close to pooling ignorance. The something more required of interdisciplinary teaching I call the practice of disciplined interloping. To enter an alien world of thought, to move within it freely without seeking premature naturalization, that is disciplined interloping.

Reflecting upon the significance of this metaphor for interdisciplinary teaching, I realize that disciplined interloping is what I try to do in *all* of my learning and teaching, even in the few areas where I claim some measure of expertise. If I lack the attitude of the interloper, I succumb to the illusion that all knowledge conforms to the paradigms which currently prevail in my area of specialization. This "premature naturalization" of knowledge, whatever its advantages, is ultimately a form of tunnel vision. In any case most of us in the humanities and the humanistically oriented social sciences inhabit what Van Harvey calls "field encompassing fields" (54-59). We employ many methods and we clothe ourselves in the working assumptions of several potentially conflicting paradigms in our acts of interloping within the realm of the unknown, the unfamiliar, or simply the dimly understood. If we speak of history, English, religious studies or a number of other disciplines, we must note that creative work is generated by the interlopers-- those who recognize that to do the work of one's field is to transgress the borders where various fields uneasily meet.

In the middle range of courses in undergraduate and graduate disciplinary programs, the centrality of interloping in skillful teaching is easily forgotten. We accustom students, instead, to put on a harness and trace the furrows of acquired knowledge across the field. This will never do, however, either at the level of the introductory undergraduate course or at that of an interdisciplinary core course in a Graduate Liberal Studies program.

At the introductory level students are usually subject to the naturalistic fallacy which assumes that my narrow range of experience with its cultural bias may be taken as the norm for how all things human are or, at least, should be. While adult learners recognize easily the diversity of the human world and operate out of divergent ways of interpreting it, they often do not know what to make of either the diversity of reality or the divergence of our forms of knowing.

In both cases, but at quite different levels in the spiral of intellectual development, to practice interloping *with* the student means recreating the kind of learning experience powerfully remembered by John Cage.

> During a counterpoint class in U.C.L.A. Schoenberg sent everybody to the blackboard. We were to solve a particular problem he had given and to turn around when finished so that he could check on the correctness of the solution. I did as directed. He said, "That's good. Now find another solution." I did. He said, "Another." Again I found one. Again he said, "Another." And so on. Finally, I said, "There are no more solutions." He said, "What is the principle underlying all of the solutions?" (93)

In some cases the course materials themselves provide the alternative solutions as in DePaul's inaugural core course, "Visions of the Self," which examines the major ways in which Western culture has construed selfhood. In other cases, as on any given evening's work with a text, it is the Graduate Liberal Studies class as a whole with its diversity of interpretations that acts the role of Cage. Only when we move past Schoenberg's final question to explore its hidden intent, however, does the full practice of interloping emerge. To discover common ground within plurality is one thing; to recognize how limited, how confined that ground really is, is another. If some framework includes the diverse "solutions," what about alternative frameworks? Here is where, to return to the example of the "Visions of the Self" course, the exploration of Hindu and Buddhist texts as a counterpoint to the models of selfhood emerging within Western cultures comes into play. In reading such a text virtually all of the students and teachers are thrown back to the basic skills of interlopers surveying an alien environment. I need to use and to help students use the generic skills of humanities disciplines for interpreting expressions of cultures quite different from our own. I need to know enough about the background and the assumptions which lie behind these texts to be able to spot the inveterate tendency of students and teachers alike to project the familiar contours of the Western world upon this alien topography. Like interlopers, we learn but do not settle; we learn to interpret and to translate without assuming that we thereby become naturalized citizens of alien worlds. Because the object of a core course like "Visions of the Self" is less an accurate comprehension of, say, Buddhist theories of the non-self than it is an attempt to fulfill Schoenberg's hidden intent, expertise which strives to make the unfamiliar familiar cedes pride of place to the learned ignorance of the disciplined interloper.

The second challenge to the teacher presented by core courses arises not from the nature of the subject matter but from typical problems of students in the courses. If we think of graduate disciplinary programs as assuming a group of students already acclimatized to the discipline, naturalized citizens as it were, Graduate Liberal Studies students, as other chapters point out, do not fit this pattern. They come to our programs usually after a relatively lengthy hiatus in formal education. More importantly, they choose Graduate Liberal Studies programs because they represent a new departure, not the unbroken continuation of previous formal or informal learning experiences. In this sense they too are committed, without always realizing it, to interloping, and the interdisciplinary focus of the core courses is eminently suited to the psychology of our new students.

Yet instructors in the core courses must be aware of the special problems that such students may face. In part the core courses need to provide an alternative to the naturalization process that disciplinary programs largely assume as accomplished. While Graduate Liberal Studies students demonstrate a raw intellectual courage and the willingness to start afresh in a new educational terrain, their break with the familiar world of professional competence also produces anxiety. A bit of patience, a few signs of reassurance are rewarded, virtually instantly, in the measurable growth of such students. A mixed audience of new students and Graduate Liberal Studies students who have taken other core courses works like a self-adjusting organism in accomplishing this task better than most faculty interventions. Anxiety also diminishes as students come into "possession of their powers." Teachers need to make such students aware that they already possess through prior experience and training many of the analytical and critical skills demanded in any graduate program. Simultaneously we need to polish rusty skills, particularly in the area of writing.

In part, faculty exercise their responsibility before they ever enter the classroom by designing the core courses to meet these needs. At DePaul each core course presents a particular and different set of writing objectives. Using a variety of written forms ranging from the intellectual journal, to short analytical and synthetic essays, to the research paper, the core program equips the student to view writing not only as a mode of communication but as a form of thinking. The core enables adult learners to see that, however painful the scraping may be, beneath the rust lies the steel that only years of experience can temper.

I have indicated that the challenges of meeting the demands of interdisciplinary learning and the needs of Graduate Liberal Studies students are not separate but related. Together an inventive Graduate Liberal Studies faculty can create coordinated ways of simultaneously addressing both kinds of challenge. In the experience of several Graduate Liberal Studies programs one such device is the use in core courses of the intellectual journal which combines analysis, comparisons, and personal reflections. In our program it has proved to be a remarkably effective tool to promote the practice of interloping, to hone writing skills, and to accustom students to the dialectic of reflection which is what we mean by learned ignorance. It epitomizes, I believe, the kinds of processes which give typical core courses in a Graduate Liberal Studies program an exploratory character as well as academic rigor, and which make them suitable to the needs of Graduate Liberal Studies students.

D. Diversity Celebrated: Teaching
Graduate Liberal Studies Students
Beyond The Core Program

The unifying regimen of the core courses gives way to a centrifugal movement as students in the middle of their programs move in a welter of directions in pursuit of highly tailored sets of intellectual objectives. Some students integrate the drive for liberal learning with a practical concern to enhance their professional lives. Others welcome the opportunity to create a program of studies unrelated to the demands of their profession. Some choose an interdisciplinary set of electives brightly focused on a particular topic area. Others weave a complicated web to capture an elusive sense of breadth. Graduate Liberal Studies programs exist to celebrate the sheer diversity of students' interests while shaping programs of study to match. Nevertheless the elective portions of students' programs creates its own set of problems for Graduate Liberal Studies faculty members.

Graduate Liberal Studies students in the elective portion of their program must be able to work well in class situations dominated by and predominantly directed to students within a particular discipline. Graduate Liberal Studies faculty can best prepare their students for this experience by developing an intense and variegated set of core learning experiences. Yet advisement which is both shaped to the individual and cognizant of the strengths and weaknesses, the possibilities and the quirks, of the institution's graduate disciplinary programs is equally essential. Not all instructors are willing to help students with intense motivation, diversified knowledge and a variety of skills but without a great deal of training in the discipline in question. Some courses preclude students with such a background. On the other hand, many faculty have approached me willing to shape their syllabi so that just such fresh minds will be attracted to their courses.

Here Graduate Liberal Studies directors and their faculty have the opportunity to broaden the impact of liberal studies programs upon the quality of instruction within the college and university. In my experience there are many more faculty with the desire and the ability to work with Graduate Liberal Studies students than there are sections of core courses for them to teach. The potential influence of liberal studies programs goes beyond directing students into the classes taught by such faculty. In most programs there is either a loosely constructed core with a large number of offerings or a tightly constructed core supplemented by a number of elective courses specifically modified to meet the intellectual concerns of Graduate Liberal Studies students. These offerings allow a wider range of faculty to integrate the purposes of liberal education with the demands of disciplinary teaching.

As I suggested earlier, such courses, with their mixed group of participants, work best when the professor moves out on a limb by applying the modes of inquiry of the discipline to a new area of investigation, thereby testing the fundamental assumptions of the discipline. So, an English professor applies the plural methods of his field to the study of autobiographical material. This offsets the graduate English student's knowledge of the discipline and its methods with the complexity and richness of experience which Graduate Liberal Studies students bring to the study of a genre that, after all, gives articulate form to the flux of experience. Or a political science professor calls into question our customary confinement of politics to a circumscribed realm by asking students to investigate the ideological content and drift, the tacit political decisions, which define our culture's communications media. In the process political science majors and Graduate Liberal Studies students alike learn something genuinely new about the social construction of reality. In each case the range of the discipline is expanded, fundamental issues central to liberal learning are raised, and new insights are generated by the juxtaposition of new materials with old approaches or the reverse.

Simultaneously, the wall of separation between faculty heavily invested in disciplinary graduate education and faculty committed to interdisciplinary exploration is breached. Suspicions, defensive postures, and plain ignorance about the common practice of teaching which we share melt away. Invariably unfounded concerns about the level of scholarship demanded in Graduate Liberal Studies programs evaporate as recognized scholars within the college work at the interesting edges of their scholarly pursuits with a mixed but all the more challenging group of students. Careful selection of faculty willing to make such adjustments, willing to pursue old questions in new formats, extends and deepens the faculty commitment to the goals of liberal studies. It also spreads what can only be called the striking zest which the faculty who create and teach the core courses share. I see this expanding reach of Graduate Liberal Studies programs, linking interdisciplinary and disciplinary teaching, in my own and other colleges as one sign of the potential of Graduate Liberal Studies programs to create a critical mass of faculty concerned about revitalizing the practice of teaching.

E. The Practice of Judgment: Teaching
Liberal Studies In A
Pluralistic Society

If we take John Cage's description of a classroom workout with Schoenberg as analogous to the group's analytical process within a Graduate Liberal Studies seminar, we can imagine a balanced emphasis among the proliferation of ideas, interpretations and arguments, the search for common ground, and the interrogation of the limits of those ideas and that ground. To accomplish that much, as Cage clearly thought, is to catapult the practice of teaching to a new level of interaction. Yet this analytical process itself eventually confronts its limits. Traditionally liberal studies focus on the ends of human life. When the ideas that we proliferate, and the common ground of assumptions that we uncover, have to do with such ends, with the central values and purposes which shape belief and action, inevitably we must ask: "But what do we make of these ideas? Are they the case?" Lonergan's spiral of the inquiring self leads to the moment of judgment as the necessary conclusion to any act of inquiry and the prelude to a further expansion of experience and understanding. It is precisely here, I suggest, that the practice of teaching in Graduate Liberal Studies programs and in the humanities and humanistically oriented social sciences in general stumbles into rough terrain.

We inhabit, Wayne Booth argues, the cultural equivalent of London's Hyde Park, where all are free to proclaim-- loudly or softly--whatever they please but where no one is listening. "Arguments for our beliefs or actions have become 'mere rhetoric' or propaganda or rationalization. Passionate commitment has lost its connection with the provision of good reasons and reason has been reduced to logical calcula- tion and proof about whatever does not matter enough to engage commitment" (Booth x-xi). The reason for this state of affairs, Booth, MacIntyre and many others hold, is the dominance of the unquestioned assumption that the ends of human life are not subject to rational discussion; our values are simply our personal preferences (Booth 3-40; MacIntyre 22-34). Ultimately, it is claimed there can be no sound versus unsound judgments or, better, sound versus sounder judgments but only opinions with which I happen to agree or disagree.

Booth and MacIntyre have taken the initiative in framing the theoretical case against this peculiarly modern dogma. My concern is with its impact upon the practice of teaching and, particularly, upon teaching within Graduate Liberal Studies programs. Bluntly put, the modern dogma insists that the spiral of experience, understanding, judgment, and decision only works when the object of the inquiry does not finally affect the meaning of human life. If Graduate Liberal Studies programs have a distinctive subject matter as well as a special audience and interdisciplinary mode of inquiry, it is precisely those ideas and values, institutions and individuals, events and movements, which do finally matter because they have shaped and may continue to shape who we are. When this dogma goes unquestioned, as it all too often does, the consequences for the classroom process in a Graduate Liberal Studies program are severe. Instead of the spiral of inquiry carried upward as a collective, mutually transforming endeavor, it twists sideways at the moment of judgment into the realm of the private, the incontestable, the unshared. Teachers and students alike enact the rituals of a *skitish pluralism,* elaborately avoiding any kind of discourse which might call into question another's beliefs or values or which might require us to take them seriously as potentially transforming our own. Convictions about the ends of human life remain sleeping dogs around which we carefully tiptoe. In this regard adult learners are simply firmer in their convictions and more adept at the etiquette of avoidance.

Clearly there are good reasons for this skitishness. A reduction of the modern Babel to a single dominant tongue is alien to one of the central values which we hold (i.e. judge) to be conducive to the genuine flourishing of human life--the value of mutual respect and tolerance. Likewise, few adults relish the war of words in which each claims the victory but no one is moved an inch. These, however, are not the only alternatives, if we follow the reasoning of thinkers like Booth, MacIntyre or Lonergan.

Beyond skitish pluralism lies what we can call *dialectical pluralism.* If the former is the consequence, in classroom and culture, of modes of inquiry and discourse grounded on the dogma that opinions about the ends of human life cannot be rationally adjudicated, the latter is the consequence of alternative modes which derive from a counter-argument that our perspectives on such ends are inevitably partial, inadequate and in need of enlargement yet comparable, often complementary and open to synthesis. If we were to base the practice of teaching on the latter premise, we would have to encourage the sense that the spiraling of experience, understanding, judgment, and decison is both unending and deeply shared. The class as a whole would have to become a microcosm of the human community as a community of inquirers.

I know of no surefire way of engaging in this practice. It involves getting articulate adults with strong convictions to listen as well as speak, to speak in ways that build upon what they have heard, to think of themselves as learning not only how to understand but to judge and, therefore, to discover that the strength of their convictions lies in their capacity for growth. It entails moving as a group from tolerant silence to respectful and mutual interrogation. Surely, it includes developing the art of synthetic reasoning in tandem with that of analysis. I believe that this practice requires disagreeing with our students while conveying clearly what we have learned from ideas which we nevertheless cannot finally hold and encouraging them to do likewise. "[T]here is no assumption here . . . that all truly reasonable men will always finally agree," concludes Booth.

> On the contrary, it is assumed that reasonable men of differing interests, experience, and vocabulary will disagree about some questions to which reason, nevertheless, must apply, . . . The supreme purpose of persuasion in this view could not be to talk someone else into a preconceived view; rather it must be to engage in mutual inquiry or exploration. In such a world, our rhetorical purpose must always be to perform as well as possible in the same primal symbolic dance, which makes us able to dance at all (111, 137).

Booth obviously has a larger practice in mind than the kind of teaching which I have argued is intrinsically related to the purposes of Graduate Liberal Studies education. Ultimately he seeks the restoration of civil discourse, a rhetoric for a pluralistic society which allows for intelligent debate about the ends of human life in this time and place. It strikes me that there is no better testing ground for Booth's proposal than a Graduate Liberal Studies class with its highly diverse gathering of articulate and intellectually committed adults.

F. Practice Restored: Graduate Liberal Studies Programs And Faculty Development

Those of us who work in and are deeply committed to Graduate Liberal Studies programs are given to messianic pretensions. It goes with the calling. Surely, the last few paragraphs should be read with that in mind and taken with a dollop of skepticism. More modestly, I wish to recapitulate in this section only how such programs can work to enhance the practice of teaching in the college at large. You may well believe that here, too, modesty has hardly overcome pretentiousness; to which I would reply--"Try it, and find out for yourself."

Graduate Liberal Studies programs do transform the teaching and professional activities of faculty in a myriad of small but tangible ways. An anthropologist who teaches a core course at DePaul called "The City" finds that the course enables him to complement his crosscultural studies of contemporary urban cultures with detailed historical studies. An English professor voices great delight in seeing his patient endeavor rewarded by enormous leaps in the writing skill of adult learners who know clearly what they do not know or cannot do and who immediately seize the opportunity to push forward. A group of four or five faculty members marvels together at what a single student in our program--a woman in her early seventies--managed to teach *us* as she moved with steady perseverance through her program of studies. Professors in various disciplines corner me in elevators and in hallways asking if Graduate Liberal Studies students would be interested in their graduate course next quarter, grateful for the change of atmosphere in a class that even two or three such students can bring. In every case one can sense the pendulum of faculty morale swing smoothly towards the positive pole.

Directors of Graduate Liberal Studies programs become collectors of such tokens of transformation. We plot the arc of the pendulum. But I have argued something more in this chapter--an essential link between the successful pursuit of the distinct goals of Graduate Liberal Studies programs and the rejuvenation of the practice of teaching. Here the effects on faculty teaching in such programs are less tangible but more decisive.

My discussion of various components of Graduate Liberal Studies programs, of demands intrinsic to that kind of curriculum as well as my occasional comments on the nature of adult learners, of their special sorts of needs and goals, evoked an image, a composite ideal, if you will, of the practice of teaching. Bernard Lonergan's understanding of intellectual transformation as a spiraling of experience, understanding, judgment, and decision; John Dewey's commitment to education as empowerment; John Cage's evocation of the imaginative and critical breakthrough demanded by his great teacher, Schoenberg; the image of the teacher as disciplined interloper; and the insistence of Wayne Booth that we make something more out of the arenas of academic and public debate than an intellectual Hyde Park. Each of these exemplars contributes something to that composite ideal. More importantly, they give concrete form to our vague sense of the goods which are internal to the practice of teaching. This juxtaposition of components of Graduate Liberal Studies programs and the composite ideal of the practice of teaching amounts then to a central claim-- Graduate Liberal Studies programs by their very nature demand and, when carefully developed, tend to elicit the virtues, that is, the habitual powers central to excellent teaching (cf. MacIntyre 178). At the same time they do expand or, at least, recall us to an underlying understanding of what those ideals, practices and virtues intrinsic to teaching really are.

If you are willing to entertain this claim as a distinct possibility, let me nudge you one final step further. As I suggested earlier, Master's programs which fall outside of professional training programs or doctoral programs constant-ly face major questions about their purpose and legitimacy. Graduate Liberal Studies programs, as each chapter of this book testifies, move beyond this impasse. If they demand and elicit excellence in the practice of teaching it goes without saying that they do likewise with the practice of learning. The pursuit of the goals of such programs is intrinsically beneficial to all who run the race. The argu-ment of this chapter, namely, that these programs *from the view of the faculty involved in them* are a distinct source of revitalization within the college or university which affects many other areas of teaching, adds simply one more reason for putting a "crisis of legitimacy" decisively behind us.

The latest of the apocalyptic pronouncements about the eclipse of the practice of teaching sits before me as I conclude this chapter. It is a recent *Doonesbury* cartoon in which a rumpled professor whose words of wisdom evoke only the scribble, scribble, scribble of dutiful notetakers resorts in desperation to verbal grenades, each more preposterous than the last. The only response is intensified scribbling. Collapsing on his lectern, he proclaims the final revelation: "Teaching is dead." Our painful, rueful smiles of recognition give evidence that Gary Trudeau has once more found his mark. But I have suggested in this chapter that it may be a too easy mark. Easier still are the attempts by the sundry committees on high education to perform the autopsy. The rumors of death, here as elsewhere, are greatly exaggerated.

I have exploited MacIntyre's "disquieting suggestion," however, because it functions as a parable, transforming our awareness of what we do, forcing us to distinguish between what is counterfeit and what is genuine coin in the practice of teaching. I find it greatly encouraging that what lives and breathes, what continues to ring true in our best work as teachers, appears to be so intimately bound to the distinct goals and purposes of Graduate Liberal Studies programs. More encouraging still is the daily evidence of the realization of the composite ideal, that complex excellence which we call the practice of teaching, in the work of teachers who pursue these goals.

Charles R. Strain, Ph.D.
De Paul University

Works Cited

Wayne Booth, *Modern Dogma and The Rhetoric of Assent* (Chicago: University of Chicago Press, 1974).

John Cage, *Silence* (Cambridge, MA: MIT Press, 1966).

Van Harvey, *The Historian and the Believer* (New York: Macmillan, 1966).

Bernard Lonergan, *Insight: A Study of Human Understanding* (New York: Harper and Row, 1958).

Alasdair MacIntyre, *After Virtue: A Study in Moral Theory* (Notre Dame, IN: University of Notre Dame Press, 1981).

DIFFERENT STUDENTS, DIFFERENT PROBLEMS, DIFFERENT SOLUTIONS

LIBERAL STUDIES IN A VARIETY OF CLASSROOMS

One encounters two remarkable features when teaching in a typical Graduate Liberal Studies program: the character of the student body and the character of the curriculum and its objectives. The experience and challenge of teaching in such a program might be best conveyed by talking about these two phenomena and their implications.

With the appearance of a large number of Graduate Liberal Studies programs, the profile of their students has emerged as an almost sociological type. The most popular phrase used to describe them is "non-traditional," which defines by exclusion; it tells us what they are not. They are not immediately post-baccalaureate, full-time, residential graduate students with salient academic or professional career goals. They are, by this definition, more typically older, part-time, with a developed array of other commitments in their lives, including job and family. Beyond these traits it may be difficult to generalize. Their ages, patterns of employment, attitudes and motivations for returning to school can vary considerably. They are, relatively speaking, a highly voluntary student population, not driven by parental or peer pressure or the pursuit of a career niche. Indeed, even before they enrolled they may have had to overcome unique barriers such as anxieties about returning to study after a long absence from the classroom or the resistance of family and friends.

For the instructor such an audience is appealing because of the diversity of backgrounds, but the initial uncertainties of these students also present certain difficulties. The instructor must continue to fulfill the classically subversive function of education in challenging conventionally acquired perspectives on the world, but in so doing he/she must be

85

prepared to discover that adult students respond to the experience with a wider range of reactions--from engaged receptivity on the one hand to real intellectual anxiety on the other. Traditional students have the security of bringing to schooling a certain continuous socialization; for the non-traditional student that thread of socialization has been interrupted and replaced by a variety of life experiences. These latter students come with a richness of background and experiences, but in need of a certain common ground or academic focus. In practical terms, I think this is greatly aided by creating, at the outset of the program, situations that help incorporate and integrate such students. In our program (at the University of Michigan-Flint), we recommend that in the very first term students take a core seminar that will consist of a relatively small number of solely Graduate Liberal Studies students. Most of our students follow this advice, continue to take courses specifically designed for the program at the beginning of their study, and postpone until later those courses which they share with other students.

Aside from the initial challenges presented by the nature of the student body, the instructor must also recognize that confronting the experience of teaching in a Graduate Liberal Studies program very much involves confronting the very traditions and values of higher education. The practical concerns involved quickly translate into larger questions of the institutional and cultural organization of intellectual activity. Formal education is structured in such a way that, as we progress, teaching increasingly involves transmitting more specialized subject matter to better prepared people. While young children confront the rudiments of language and mathematics and the shape of the world, young adults study fluid mechanics and Baroque art. The denouement of this enterprise is the research doctorate in which biologists choose what bacteria to study, literature scholars pick their favorite author, and social scientists find two things that never before have been correlated. Professional graduate education, though guided by a focus on practice, leads essentially in the same direction. The progress of knowledge is challenging not for its integration but by virtue of the unrelenting thoroughness of such specialization required to break new ground and create new knowledge. Disciplines and fields are defined as much by what one does not have to know to pursue them, i.e., by what they aggressively exclude. Scholarly research depends on a certain concentration of the mind and a focusing of energies. It is certainly the convention of our culture that knowledge advances by way of this linear progression of knowing more about less.

Given the convention, the movement to develop broad-based liberal studies programs at the graduate level seems jarring and may be met with suspicion. It also poses real challenges for students with undergraduate backgrounds which reflect definite concentrations and majors, and in which the least articulated and defended element was "general education." It poses similar challenges for faculty who hold specialized research doctorates. Such a curriculum may seem less strange if we recognize that the linear hierarchy of knowledge is, in fact, neither a fair nor a comprehensive rendering of the progress of knowledge. Indeed, the progress of knowledge might be viewed as more circular, for out of specialization, ideally, higher stages of integration and broader constructions of understanding and insight are derived. It is the reintegration of the specialized that gives the specialty its import and makes it part of larger intellectual discourse. While specialization results from the exigencies of moving new knowledge forward and while it is institutionally valued, it does not thereby constitute a definition of what advanced study is. Though in the past interdisciplinary work has been suspect, even if periodically fashionable, it has come to be increasingly accepted as a critical approach to advanced research. For example, the University of Michigan, through a program called "Presidential Initiatives," recently allocated $1.2 million to fund a number of interdisciplinary and integrative scholarly projects involving diverse teams of faculty from many disciplines. Interdisciplinarity is no longer just a device for creating undergraduate courses that sound interesting but a fundamental movement in academia that perhaps represents an inevitable response to a situation in which the Balkanization of disciplines and sub-fields has served to constrain their power and impact.

Designing an appropriate curriculum for, and teaching in, interdisciplinary studies at the graduate level involves confronting such basic issues about the underlying assumptions and organization of formal education. Since I would like to link some of these observations to my own experience as a faculty member in a Graduate Liberal Studies program, I should explain a bit the particulars of that experience. I have been involved with a thirty-credit program consisting of a required set of four "core seminars," a series of electives drawn from a number of departmental courses, and a thesis. Our program is somewhat distinctive in that it has a particular thematic focus on American Culture. The four core seminars, the heart of the program in a sense, are designed around certain major themes in American Culture that are examined in an interdisciplinary manner. The departmental electives, which are open both to advanced undergraduate students and, with additional work as a requirement, to graduate students, are essentially discipline-based courses that are related to the study of American culture.

The most challenging teaching generally is that which is broad and integrative. At the undergraduate level, it is the introductory course more than the advanced course that can be the most demanding. The integrative demands of pedagogy in Graduate Liberal Studies programs call upon students not just to know certain things but to use what they know and to relate it to other areas of information and knowledge. In this regard it is interesting to note the extent to which students--even those who as undergraduates have majored in the liberal arts--come to the program with a fairly well developed discipline orientation. A Graduate Liberal Studies program may be thought of as delaying or impeding the specialization characteristic of graduate education but, in fact, experience suggests that a great deal of focusing has already set in, and this can be seen in the difficulties of confronting an integrative curriculum. Students seem to come to the program with a certain repertoire of background and skills that make them comfortable with parts of the interdisciplinary mix, but threatened by other parts. One practical response to this has been to employ thematically linked materials that represent different disciplinary styles and analytical approaches. The diversity should provide each student with an intellectual "home" from which to reach out to less familiar terrain.

Another manifestation of this challenge appears in the area of writing ability and the approach to research. Even among students who write very well, what is found in the classroom is a very eclectic mix of styles, approaches and expectations reflecting a variety of undergraduate concentrations. The undergraduate literature major writes expressive critique, the social scientist writes empirical analysis, and so forth. Similarly, research itself takes on various meanings with such a diverse audience, depending on whether the student's background is more in literature, history, philosophy or social science. Assignments in which students personally select their topics tend to relieve this problem; in addition, such assignments permit students to link the integrative field to their own interests and strengths. This is not necessarily a good approach, however. The most common pitfall is that students tend to use such opportunities to retreat to the relative safety of what they know already. Thus, common writing assignments may be better; they tend to confront this problem directly and, while they may prove more demanding, ideally they can be used to explore and articulate a common, shared focus of intellectual activity.

A particularly interesting situation arises in regard to our "departmental" courses that serve, in effect, as disciplinary courses to an interdisciplinary audience. The understandable difficulty with such a course is that the graduate students may seem unevenly prepared for this level of work if their undergraduate background in the specific field is lacking. In our program, for example, it is important to recognize that the "expertise" they bring to the department elective is not that of the discipline but of the liberal studies theme of American culture. While the problem often is viewed as one of the student's preparation, it may just as well indicate flaws in the design and objectives of the course, for one of the objectives should involve relating focused disciplinary study to the liberal studies program. That is to say, the additional readings and assignments required of Graduate Liberal Studies students in these courses should serve not just as opportunities to add appropriate rigor, but to help bridge the dual mission of the course. For example, while political science majors in a course on American political thought might be devoting attention to the relation of ideas to political processes, the Graduate Liberal Studies students might appropriately direct their attention to the relationship between such ideas and other intellectual currents in American culture. This example is not intended to indicate a formal or rigid division along these lines but to demonstrate the legitimacy of a course's dual role.

What this small example does indicate is the need for a sense of the identity and central purpose of liberal studies that is sufficiently articulate and strong to offset the magnetic attraction of disciplinary expertise. Without this there is a sense of "watering down" graduate education, a tendency to interpret a different mission as a lesser mission. The ability of interdisciplinary study to provide this core purpose and meaning is best understood by looking at one of the commitments and potential flaws of disciplinary study.

Disciplines are dedicated to the notion that aspects of human experience and reality can be examined in isolation from others; reality is studied by breaking it up. But this legitimate terrain for expertise does not alter the contextual and holistic character of reality. Disciplinary work runs into intellectual traps when it begins to forget this. What interdisciplinary inquiry offers is an awareness of the continuity of reality, a recognition that there is a limit to understanding things analytically separate.

Yet it is equally important to keep in mind that the tension between disciplinary and interdisciplinary is a somewhat artificial and fairly recent historical phenomenon. Important disciplinary work is not narrowly isolated or necessarily constrained by method. Serious inquiry from any one field does not ignore the interconnections with neighboring fields, and great thinkers, scientists and writers of the past defy easy categorization according to today's fields of study. Disciplines, ideally, offer opportunities for inquiry; they are not supposed to be intellectual ghettos.

Despite the growing acceptance of broadly based graduate study, a certain anxiety about interdisciplinarity is common in contemporary academia and often produces somewhat stilted and mechanical conceptions. Typical is the course description which promises an "artistic, literary, historical, social, political and economic study of . . ." I think it is a pretense to configure the task of interdisciplinary study in such a way that a person who has solid training in a discipline could not possibly be expected to succeed in it. It would be much more constructive to begin thinking about the mission of interdisciplinary curricula in more minimalist terms. A simple, if undramatic, premise is that interdisciplinary study is non-disciplinary. Even this minimalist standard contains a powerful shift of perspective and approach, for it means a shift in emphasis from the integrity of method to the integrity of questions. It suggests more a process of reaching out than a process of patching together different points of view. An exciting intellectual challenge involves discovering how one's disciplinary home fits into the world at large.

It is likely to be the case that Graduate Liberal Studies will seem to be one of the most innovative and unusual as well as one of the most traditional programs on campus. The program may suggest an innovative and daring approach, counter to the conventions of graduate education. Yet the curriculum is rooted in classical forms and conceptions of higher education; a most traditional commitment to learning and intellectual growth prevails; and the students are becoming increasingly more typical of the student body in general on American college and university campuses (by 1992, if present projections hold true, half of all students in colleges and universities in the United States will be over twenty-five years old). If there is a central challenge in teaching liberal studies it is the challenge of rediscovering and asserting the value of our intellectual roots.

William Meyer, Ph.D.
University of Michigan-Flint

THE PARTICULAR PROBLEMS
OF SCIENCE FOR HUMANISTS

A great many of the students enrolled in Graduate Liberal Studies programs are unskilled in science. This is hardly a matter for surprise. The low level of scientific literacy has been noted countless times, and the observations of people like C. P. Snow continue to be accurate assessments of the educational scene. Indeed, Norriss S. Hetherington in a recent piece discussing the relative prominence of America and Japan in our technological world stresses the American student's lack of scientific knowledge.[1] Students in the humanities are woefully ignorant of even the most basic body of scientific thought and technique. The matter is in many ways exacerbated by the kinds of courses that are offered to undergraduate non-science students to fulfill their general education requirements in science. Faculty try hard to introduce some substance into these courses, but the very existence of the courses themselves is a surrender to the mindset that claims that some chosen few have an aptitude for science, and the rest are beyond hope.

Only in sciences do we seem to accept this elitist and defeatist attitude. Introductory humanities and social science

91

courses do not distinguish between majors and non-majors. There isn't a watered down poetry class for chemists; they are expected to deal with metaphor and allusion. Why aren't English majors expected to understand oxidation-reduction reactions?

My own training is both humanistic and scientific. I have a doctorate in philosophy and have done graduate work in biochemistry. I appreciated the opportunity to put those two worlds together in a Graduate Liberal Studies course. I also thought there was a real necessity to do so. Shelley was a world-class chemist, and his easy familiarity with the world of molecules enlivens his poetry. Kant knew a great deal about physics and astronomy; Goethe speculated brilliantly about botanical metamorphosis. In the twentieth century science and technology have exploded, and there is a danger that we are abandoning the fruitful cross-fertilization that marked the previous centuries.

I would claim that two myths reinforce the divisions between science and humanities. The first is that the technical, mathematical language of science makes it impenetrable without special aptitude and years of study. The second is that there is an objectivity to science, a rightness and wrongness to answers, that sets it apart from the subjective considerations of the arts and humanities. While there is considerable truth to both these ideas, they present an overly simplified picture of the scientific enterprise, and one that preserves the gulf between science and humanities.

The idea that the literature of science can be read only by scientists must be challenged. With some background and some patience, non-scientists can learn to read technical literature with adequate comprehension. Indeed, non-scientists *must* learn to read it. Many questions of more than merely scientific importance turn on technical matters. Humane interests are not served by relying exclusively on technicians to decide questions like the legal definition of death or the uses and limits of genetic engineering.

Similarly, the perception that science alone gives objective certainty must be called into question. The certainty of science exists at the level of established knowledge and not at the limits of research. The science we teach in the schools is usually the litany of what is known. The sense that science has definite right and wrong answers comes mainly from this practice. I think it is important to remember that, at the elementary level, the humanities are just as secure and have just as strong a claim to right and wrong answers. In language, rules of spelling, grammar and syntax have precisely the same level of certainty as do laws of reflection in optics. When one moves beyond the conventional and established, whether in literature or in biochemistry, the ideal of objective truth is less clearly obtainable.

This was to be a major theme in the course I planned to teach. The students were to grow familiar with science in a way that would build bridges between the activity of the scientist and the work of the humanist. They were to come away from the course respectful of science but less in awe of it; they were to have an understanding of its level of uncertainty and of its adventure.

There is a challenge to designing a course for a Graduate Liberal Studies program that addresses the scientific component of the modern world. One certainly cannot understand or appreciate the present century unless one is attuned to the revolutionary excitement of modern science. But there are a number of areas to choose from, and a number of events or themes that are appropriate. Ours is the age of quantum mechanics and psychotherapy, of computers and evolutionary theory. There is so much to know, and any one of a hundred topics would provide an adequate backbone for a course designed to give some insight into the interplay of science in contemporary life and thought.

In some ways the easiest course to design and teach would be one that used evolutionary biology as the central theme. I could assign Darwin's *Origin of Species* without any hesitation. Evolution and social darwinism have an important place in twentieth-century intellectual history. Recent legal attacks by fundamentalist groups have generated some nice essays on what is scientific theory and what is not. The debate within the scientific community concerning punctuated evolution showed the field to be a fertile one for continued intellectual speculation.

As sensible as this approach seemed to be, I chose not to teach it. One reason was probably sheer perversity. Evolution was too easy: it was descriptive, I could avoid mathematical and chemical equations, people knew a lot about it already. Other reasons were my own interests and my belief that investigations more important than those centering on evolution were guiding the direction of biological research. I preferred molecules to animal populations, and a science that was more directly and immediately experimental.

Not quite one hundred years after Darwin and Wallace published the preliminary version of the theory of natural selection, Watson and Crick produced an equal stir by elucidating the structure of the DNA molecule. So I chose to design a course for non-scientists based on what Watson called the molecular biology of the gene.

I had still another reason. I wanted to show that in some of the best scientific research there is a sense of adventure, and of drama. Not all projects are fortunate enough to have those qualities--a great deal of important progress is incremental--but the story of disparate pieces fitting together because someone developed a fruitful theoretical approach is a good story. The work on the molecular biology of the gene is that kind of story, and it has often been told that way.

There is also the fact that a lot of the work, especially after Watson and Crick, was guided by what Crick called "the central dogma of molecular biology"; namely, that DNA makes RNA makes protein. This was the image, the *idee fixe*, that directed a great deal of the research on the genetic code. I wanted my students to see how an idea or theme, a kind of scientific obsession, could drive experimental and theoretical research. This was not the objective scientist systematically proceeding along the preordained path of knowledge. This was a group of men passionately committed to a hunch--a tremendously fruitful hunch, as it turned out, but also one that turned out to be true in only a very qualified way.

Then, too, there was the wonderful fact that with DNA, anyway, the congruence between structure and function was evident. In their first paper in *Nature*, Watson and Crick said: "It has not escaped our notice that the specific pairing we have postulated immediately suggests a possible copying mechanism for the genetic material."[2] The fact that the mechanical structure of the molecule (in essence its shape, the double helix) provided a possible picture of how it could replicate, as the gene must do, was strong evidence for the accuracy of the model. In a sense the relation between structure and function was a given in this work. Watson and Crick simply took it to be supporting evidence because they could easily imagine the two strands of the molecule separating, unwinding, and then rebuilding their missing halves. I could ask my students why this made the model so convincing.

Like Crick's "central dogma," the structure-function relation has more to do with what we want the world to be,

94

with our intuitions of the order of nature, than with any scientifically established fact. And in an important way, it highlights the presence of metaphor in science. At the very sophisticated level of the structure of molecules, we are picturing shapes that fit together like jigsaw puzzles, or open like zippers. At this point the gulf between the humanities and the sciences is not very wide at all.

Finally, what was in many ways most interesting and important to me was the faith implicit in all this work that the answers to the most perplexing questions of the life sciences lay within the molecules that comprised the living organisms. One of the perennial debates in the speculative literature that links philosophy and biology for the past hundred years[3] is the reductionist question: is biology finally chemistry? are the complex behavioral responses of our lives nothing more than the way in which chemicals in the brain attach to cells and stimulate or suppress certain biochemical reactions? I wanted to raise that question with my students in a dramatic way, because questions of free will, responsibility, and personal identity hang in the balance.

For these reasons the molecular biology of the gene was a more interesting topic than evolutionary biology. But these very reasons complicated my teaching task. I was dealing with students whose last serious brush with chemistry was in high school, and who, if they thought about biological molecules at all, thought about them in terms of the latest mouthwash commercial on television. I needed them to be comfortable with at least some of the chemical terminology because before the course was over I wanted them to look at the technical literature. I thought it was important for them to read some of the classical research papers in the field.

The subject was suited to an easy introduction. The material was so important that it was given a strong play in the popular press. Not only did journals like *Scientific American* carry numerous articles tracing the developments in the field, but newspapers like *The New York Times* and magazines like *Time* and *Newsweek* featured stories on the latest discoveries and speculations. I used this popular literature as an introduction. There were two initial assignments. The first was to find a recent story or article that was tied to DNA. It could be about new discoveries in the field, or about projected benefits to be reaped, or about potential dangers or ethical dilemmas. I wanted to make it clear that this was an ongoing topic--one that affected not just the scientific community but ordinary citizens. The second assignment was to go back in the popular and semi-popular press to the time shortly after the initial work to see how the discoveries were reported and described.

As the major texts of the class we used Horace Freeland Judson's *The Eighth Day of Creation* and James A. Watson's *The Double Helix.* Judson's book is an excellent, detailed account of the whole constellation of scientists and research associated with molecular genetics in the fifties and sixties. Watson's book is a very idiosyncratic account of his own and Francis Crick's work on the structure of DNA. Although Judson's book is written for a lay audience, it sets forth the science in careful detail, and my students found it very difficult to understand.

There were several problems which I tried to solve. One is simply that without some background in biochemistry the terminology is threatening and relationships are unclear. Amino acids, nucleic acids, proteins, pentose sugar back-bones--what in the world was going on here? I spent a lot of class time providing the basic information. Judson and Watson were describing their work from their point of view; I was trying to say some of the same things from a slightly different perspective. I relied often on metaphor. Because I was not training scientists, I thought I could sacrifice some of the precision of scientific thought. I was willing, for example, to use laundry detergent commercials with little PacMan-like creatures eating stains to describe proteolytic enzymes.

There is the inherent difficulty here of striking the right balance between the accuracy of the information and the accessibility of the image. And there is the further difficulty that the science itself uses metaphor to guide research. (When protein biochemists explain the selective binding of a ligand to a receptor as a "lock-and-key mechanism," we are already several imaginative layers removed from the quantum mechanical events taking place.) There is no easy way to avoid these difficulties, and the class was no doubt uncertain about how seriously to take the images and illustrations. A lot of caveats were necessary, but in the long run I believe the students developed a feel for the material.

Another problem is that science goes on in a laboratory, and it is a long distance from the laboratory procedure to the published research paper, let alone to the popular account. I used the biochemistry lab for some classes and did demonstrations. The most successful demonstration class was a DNA extraction. It was good theater because at the end of the extraction procedure the DNA precipitates out of solution in long white filaments that can be wrapped around a stirring rod like cotton candy. All of a sudden the process that we had been drawing diagrams of and talking about in technical terms had a perceptible existence. More important for the class, however, was the experience of watching a biochemical procedure, seeing some of the equipment at work, appreciating the time involved (the extraction takes about four hours) and the painstaking precision of the work. It was also important for the class to appreciate that the neat diagrams that appear in both technical and popular journals are highly abstract and theoretical descriptions of the work of the lab; they are ways of picturing the events, and as such are imaginative creations.

The most ambitious assignment for the class, and the one that was least successful, was the requirement to select an original research paper from a technical journal related to the work we were discussing, and report on its contents. I told the class not to spend time puzzling over the "Materials and Methods" section, but to read the rest of the article carefully and several times. Study the data to see whether it really says what the author claims in the "Results" section. Pay attention to the "Conclusion," where, often as not, the researcher tells you where he thinks the work is heading and what he expects the long-term consequences to be. With the advantage of twenty years of additional history, you can see how prescient scientists are.

I hoped that by the end of the semester the students would be familiar enough with the terminology, and comfortable enough with the overall project of molecular genetics, to read, and make some sense of, a paper like that of Monod, Jacob, and Changeux's on the lac-operon. In fact, for the most part, they could not. The course had not demystified biochemistry to the point where they could handle the literature and make an educated guess about its worth. This mistake, however, was only pedagogical. I underestimated the opacity of the material because of my own familiarity with it. What I needed, and failed, to do was to provide the class with two or three key papers and examine them as part of the classroom work instead of turning them loose on the literature and expecting them to puzzle it out.

How successful overall was the course? Near the close of the semester, after class, a group of us were talking.

One of the students, who was a high school civics teacher, told the story of having been asked in class by his students, who had just come from biology, if he knew what DNA was. "And I told them," he said, "all about base pairs, about purines and pyrimidines, and sugar phosphate backbones, and hydrogen bonds. They were very impressed, and so was I. I really knew what I was talking about."

I would hesitate to claim that this story proves the success of the course, though it does suggest a small triumph. Like any teaching experiment, this one had elements that worked and elements that did not. The students did not reach a point where they felt comfortable with the straight work of molecular genetics as reported in scientific journals. On the other hand, I think they acquired a knowledge of how science goes on, and what kinds of judgments and decisions and interpretations scientists make in the course of their work. The role of subjectivity was, I hope, more obvious at the end of the course. They could see the use the scientist made of imagery, metaphor and the like for understanding biochemical events. And they did learn that the work of the scientist can be, and must be, accessible to the non-scientist, who must ultimately have a say in what is to be done with the work.

Frank J. Cunningham, Ph.D.
Loyola College in Maryland

Endnotes

1. Norriss S. Hetherington, "British Empire's Sad Lesson for America," *The Wall Street Journal,* Thursday, December 31, 1987.

2. *Nature* (25 April 1953) 171: 737-738.

3. Cf., for instance, Bergson's *Creative Evolution,* Teilhard de Chardin's *The Phenomenon of Man,* Koestler and Smythies' *Beyond Reductionism.*

STUDENT PROFILES AND DEMOGRAPHIC TRENDS

A review of the curriculum of the more than sixty Graduate Liberal Studies programs, labelled variously as the Master of Arts in Liberal Studies, Master of Liberal Studies, Master of Humanities, Master of Modern Studies, or Master of Social Sciences, indicates that despite a diversity of design and nomenclature, two major objectives of these programs are to provide an interdisciplinary approach to learning and to stimulate intellectual excitement without necessarily aiming at particular professional trainings.[1]

The faculty who teach in these programs usually are attracted by the opportunity to teach an interdisciplinary course either alone or as part of a team. They are able to expand their own intellectual horizons, experiment with an innovative curriculum not permissible in traditional programs, and teach a highly motivated group of diversified learners who come with different academic and life experiences.

Yet, as interesting as a curriculum and faculty may be, they need a student population to sustain them. Many of the programs were in fact initiated only after market surveys were conducted among currently enrolled undergraduates, the alumni, and the neighboring community in order to ascertain the potential interest in a liberal studies curriculum. It is important both for students seeking an appropriate graduate program and administrators contemplating the establishment of such interdisciplinary programs to know the kinds of students who enroll in them. Therefore, some of the questions addressed in this chapter are:

1. Why are students attracted to a Graduate Liberal Studies program?
2. What is the characteristic student profile personally and professionally?
3. How do the goals of the students mesh and match with the mission statements of the various colleges and universities which offer these programs?
4. Do students enter with certain goals in mind, but derive other satisfactions in the process?

99

5. Which courses did students particularly enjoy and what are the implications of their preferences?
6. What have currently enrolled students as well as graduates accomplished personally and professionally as a result of the Graduate Liberal Studies program?
7. What is the prognosis for the future enrollment in such programs?[2]

Mission Statements: What Are They Telling The Applicant?

Interest in these Graduate Liberal Studies programs is often generated by the mission statements of the college or university in its brochure and bulletin. Of course, once a program has been properly advertised and has been in existence for any length of time, its continued success will be largely dependent on the sustained quality of the program and the word-of-mouth recommendation of its students.

Following is a brief list of the mission statements of some Graduate Liberal Studies programs:

1. to provide a multidisciplinary approach designed for "mature learners established in a career or profession who wish to enrich their personal lives, to explore areas of knowledge that were bypassed in the earlier rush to prepare for a career and/or to pursue an avocation in a disciplined fashion" (De Paul University, Illinois);

2. "to provide balance to specialization" (Baker University, Missouri);

3. "to provide a curriculum that is both structured and flexible for individuals who want to engage in both directed and independent work on subjects that are not bound by the curricula of traditional disciplines" (Dartmouth College, New Hampshire);

4. "to provide an interdisciplinary approach to the value system of both occidental and oriental cultures" (Grambling State University, Louisiana);

5. to provide an "interdisciplinary program that stresses the interrelatedness of the liberal arts disciplines" that

will "enable individuals not only to enrich their personal lives but to deepen the understanding with which they engage in professional, civic, interpersonal and avocational decision-making" (Hamline University, Minnesota);

6. to present an interdisciplinary approach that draws its strengths from the Humanities, Fine Arts and Social Studies for students who wish to build "an integrated program in conformity with their intellectual interests and their personal needs" (Hollins College, Virginia);

7. to provide a graduate degree "which is interdisciplinary in nature and nonprofessional in intent. It is not designed to train participants for a specific vocation but to foster the personal intellectual growth that is an asset in any field" (Lake Forest College, Illinois);

8. "to make the liberal arts more accessible to adults from all walks of life--teaching, journalism, law, medicine, social work, business, government, industry--by meeting the special interests and needs of those already established in their chosen vocations" (Louisiana State University at Shreveport);

9. to present a program on the twentieth century in America, "including the roots of that experience as they are found in other times and cultures" (Loyola College in Maryland);

10. to provide a program dealing with "great works" in a format largely of discussion rather than lecture since the relationship between students and tutors is viewed as a cooperative enterprise (St. John's University, New Mexico);

11. to provide a cluster of courses related by theme or subject (State University of New York at Stony Brook);

12. to provide a program that "can serve as suitable preparation for careers in publishing, communications, arts administration, advertising; [this program] offers a diverse urban population the opportunity for an individualized self-enrichment program at the graduate level" (University of Colorado at Denver).

Although I have cited some of the missions of only a dozen of the institutions which offer Graduate Liberal Studies programs, these statements are characteristic of the entire range of the interdisciplinary liberal arts programs offered. It is obvious that sudents who enroll in these programs are made aware that the primary objective is, for the most part, not a specific kind of professional training. Nonetheless, the student may be inspired to seek a new profession, receive a promotion as a result of an advanced level of graduate training, receive teacher certification, or obtain a salary differential. It is also clear that most of these programs offer flexibility, if not in every aspect of the curriculum, usually in the selection of electives that either are from more than one discipline or are interdisciplinary in content, and in the choice of final project, which need not be a conventional thesis. These programs are scheduled in the evenings or on weekends, sometimes exclusively during summer sessions (primarily for a large teacher population), and are conceived largely as part-time programs to accommodate the working adult.

Adult Criteria And Student Enrollment

Beyond the mission statements of the institutions, the admissions criteria are the initial instruments for student selection. Consequently, a brief review of the general admissions requirements is in order. These fall into five categories: academic index; graduate record examinations; autobiographical essay; letters of recommendation; personal interview.

Eight percent of the Graduate Liberal Studies programs require an undergraduate G.P.A. of 2.5 or better out of a possible 4.0; twelve percent require a 2.75 index or better; thirty-one percent require a 3.0 index or better; forty-six percent require a Bachelor of Arts or Science degree from an accredited institution; three percent require a Bachelor of Arts or Science degree with no particular index restriction for provisional acceptance, but do require at least six credits of B work on the graduate level either in the program or in other bona fide graduate programs.

Fifteen percent of the institutions require graduate record examinations. However, most institutions, recognizing the large interval between undergraduate and graduate education for most of their applicants, dispense with the graduate record examinations but rely on other criteria to assess verbal and writing skills as well as general preparation for graduate work. The institutions that do require the examinations also indicate that their applicants tend to be more recent undergraduates.

Twenty-seven percent require an autobiographical essay that includes the prospective student's motivation for enrolling in the program. This essay also serves as an indicator of the applicant's ability to express himself or herself in an articulate manner. Difficulty with writing skills usually shows up in this essay.

Fifty percent require at least two letters of recommendation either from faculty members of the institution from which the student received degrees or from employers or others wishing to attest to the abilities and character of the applicant. Although such letters might seem perfunctory, they frequently shed light on the motivation of the candidate and also on any discrepancies that might appear in the undergraduate transcript, such as uneven performance.

Ninety-nine percent require a personal interview either with the director of the program or with a counselor affiliated with the program. This interview helps the director determine whether the applicant will be able to function well with the other students in the group. Since classes are small and independent study and tutorials play an important part in the curriculum, the personality factor is more important here than it is in a lecture format. It is also at this time that the director learns what kinds of projects might interest the student, what kinds of electives might be of interest, and whether the curriculum will satisfy the needs of the student. Some programs are more structured than others. Should a student be looking for a self-learning model or total flexibility, a highly structured program will not be a good match.

Program directors are aware that academic index on entry will not by itself be a sufficient indicator of probable performance in the program, and they rely substantially on both the autobiographical essay and interview to determine the eligibility of applicants.

During the application process, applicants learn the academic requirements for completing the degree. Most institutions require maintenance of a B average over 30-36 credits of course work and allow no more than 7-9 credits of C work. Therefore, to a certain extent, self-selection also enters into the evaluation.

Recruitment Of Students

Where do Graduate Liberal Studies students come from? When queried about the percentage of applicants who were local residents, fifty-eight percent of the institutions surveyed said ninety-five to one hundred percent; twenty-three percent said seventy-five to ninety percent; fifteen percent said twenty-nine to fifty percent. The latter group consisted largely of institutions that run their programs principally in the summer.

Since a number of institutions rely heavily on alumni for enrollment (and new programs frequently believe that they should), it is interesting to note that fifty percent of the institutions surveyed had under five percent of their enrollment from alumni. Thirty-eight percent had ten to forty percent; four percent had forty-one to eighty-four percent; eight percent had eighty-five to one hundred percent. What accounts for the overall low alumni enrollment? At institutions where most of the alumni had not been local residents, it is unlikely that the alumni would return for this kind of master's degree. Institutions that drew their student body from the local area for the undergraduate degree are more likely to continue to attract these graduates to other degree programs; this is particularly true for institutions that had special undergraduate programs for the older adult student.

Seventy-nine percent of the institutions surveyed said that ninety to one hundred percent of their students had studied exclusively at a four-year college rather than at a combination of two-year plus four-year college; sixteen percent had seventy-five to eighty-nine percent; and five percent had fifty-nine to seventy-four percent. These statistics may mean that applicants are more likely to be students who initially selected a liberal arts college and wish to continue the same kind of education. Most students who initially selected a community college may be more likely to seek graduate programs that are more job-related.

Enrollment patterns vary from college to college. Georgetown University, which had eighteen students in its first class in 1974, now has one hundred students. Wesleyan University, the first institution to offer an MLA program, had about three hundred students in 1973 and that figure has now doubled, although in the 1960's there had been a slump

104

in enrollment. The State University of New York at Stony Brook, which began its master's program in 1967 with a little over one hundred students, now enrolls almost three thousand, most of whom are teachers.[3] Most programs in urban areas admit anywhere from ten to twenty-five students per semester; most residential colleges admit six to ten students per semester. Those colleges that offer a summer session as the primary time frame for their program have a higher number of enrollments during that period. Among the latter are Dartmouth College and Wesleyan University. The schools with the largest number of students either have a large number of teachers in their program or offer fewer master's degree programs at their institution or have little competition in their geographic area.

The age distribution of students in these programs is as follows:

Ages 21-30	26%
31-40	40%
41-50	21%
51+	13%

The ratio of women to men is on the average sixty-five percent to thirty-five percent. The higher number of women may be attributed to two major factors: the changes in demographic trends nationally and the professional background of the applicants. "In 1966 only 29 percent of the college entrants over the age of 21 were women; by 1978 women constituted 57 percent of the older freshmen," reports K. Patricia Cross in her book, *Adults as Learners*.[4] A larger pool of women would have been eligible for graduate programs by 1984. Moreover, more women than men are in the teaching profession, and thirty percent of the institutions indicate that fifty percent or more of their students come from the teaching profession. In certain states, teacher certification may be earned with this degree or teachers may apply the degree to the requirements for either the first or second salary differential.

The primary intention of the earliest established programs was to provide a general liberal arts education to students who might not have had the opportunity to have a broad-based education at the undergraduate level. The programs were directed initially to applicants who had majored in elementary education, business and science. Yet, a review of the data of many of these institutions makes it apparent that the audience is somewhat different than the one intended. Of the thirty institutions that responded to the survey, the breakdown by undergraduate major in the program is as follows: forty-one percent had majored in Humanities (English was the predominate subject); thirty-eight percent in the Social Sciences (included in this category are business and history; five percent had majored in economics or business); eight percent in the sciences; six percent in education (high school teachers were listed by their primary discipline rather than by education); seven percent in the Arts (including art, communications, dance, film, music, television/radio, and theater). These students are frequently employed in middle management positions, regardless of their undergraduate major. But approximately seventy-nine percent of students who enroll in these Graduate Liberal Studies programs had at least 32 credits of general liberal studies subjects and had even specialized in liberal studies disciplines. Rather than lacking a background in liberal studies, many of these students selected the program because it afforded them the opportunity to resume an intellectual experience that had been attractive to them at the undergraduate level. However, most deemed their contact with the liberal studies either insufficient in certain aspects or simply too remote after a hiatus of five to ten or more years from formal learning; they were interested in updating their knowledge or exploring certain subjects in greater depth and from a larger perspective.

This type of program allows some students the occasion to get their feet wet in order to see if they are intellectually able to pursue more professionally oriented degrees or simply to return to an intellectually stimulating environment that complements their vocational and/or private life.

STUDENT PROFILES; STUDENT GOALS

Whereas institutional mission statements and statistical data regarding the student population provide a broad view of the enrollment picture in Graduate Liberal Studies programs, the particular student cases, revealed through the responses of students in representative programs to a questionnaire concerning their motivation, objectives, expectations, likes and dislikes, and accomplishments, convey some of the nuances in the motivation of students to enroll in and graduate from these programs, thereby providing a more complete student profile.[5] Although each student

106

provides only his or her reason(s) for enrolling in the program, the administrators concur that these profiles are representative of other students in their respective programs.

Stanley Dorman, a student in the Master of Liberal Arts program at The Johns Hopkins University School of Continuing Studies, reported that he had a rather unsuccessful career as a student at the University of Maryland, directly following high school. He left the university as a junior because he disliked business courses, and he was "unfortunately a business major." After his return to Baltimore, his marriage and his involvement in the family business, he returned to college in 1973 at the age of thirty-three, enrolling in The Johns Hopkins Evening School's undergraduate program, where he obtained a bachelor's degree in philosophy in 1977. In the course of his undergraduate career he had encountered a professor who taught a course entitled "Existentialism and the Thriller." Mr. Dorman said that "the workload was awesome for one newly married and newly in a business career. . . ." The result was that he received a C grade, but had an exchange with the professor that made him reflect on his abilities and on his attitude toward life. At a later period, during the course of a cocktail party, he learned that the professor who had made him question his abilities was now a neighbor and would be teaching a course the following fall in The Johns Hopkins University's MLA program. He believed that if he were to regain his self-esteem and if his search for meaning in life were real, then he needed "to confront [the professor] in the classroom." He added, "That's why I enrolled in the MLA program." This latter explanation was in a letter appended to his questionnaire, in which he originally listed as his first reason for enrolling, "primarily to broaden my understanding of literature and history."

Mr. Dorman's undergraduate career is typical of the careers of many adult students, and his enrollment in the program, while having a broad objective, was triggered by a particular professor's impact on his sense of self and his desire to continue his search for meaning in life. Even for students who are not initially attracted by a professor, faculty involvement with the student while in the program often plays an important role in retention and completion of the degree.

Mr. Thomas Knowlton of Dartmouth College was interested in going to school only during the summer session to take courses which he "had neglected to take while in college." Moreover, he was considering a career in teaching and would need a Master's degree to qualify. He said, "I learned a good deal about political philosophy and U.S. history, two areas in which my [undergraduate] course selections were scanty."

Mr. Frank Reichert of Baker University in Missouri wished to broaden his horizons in liberal arts, especially since earlier studies were in science and theology. He thought this program would enhance his ministry. He particularly enjoyed a course entitled "The Physiology of Positive Aging."

In the cases of Mr. Knowlton and Mr. Reichert, this degree program enabled them to supplement their undergraduate education and to balance their specializations. At The Johns Hopkins University, Dr. Christian Mass wished to widen his knowledge in fields both related and unrelated to his career in Occupational Medicine. He also wanted to keep himself intellectually active after the age of sixty. He was contemplating publishing articles, and this degree, he maintained, would be helpful in his non-medical activities. The final project he was involved with was entitled "The Image of the Worker in Art." Courses he particularly enjoyed were: "Men and Work"; "The Age of Jackson"; "France from World War II to the Present"; and "Renaissance Art." Dr. Mass's diversity of course selection is typical of many students' programs. One can also see how these courses contributed to his choice of final project.

Jane Tolbert, at Moorhead State University, Minnesota, a training specialist in a hospital, working in managerial and staff development, enjoyed "the stimulation of studying and discussing current issues with friends." This desire to foster a new social milieu was cited by a number of students as one of the reasons for coming into the program. It is not uncommon that students in these programs are at various transitions in their lives: divorce, separation from grown children; choosing a new career; retirement.

Format is also an important factor in the adult student's enjoyment of the program. Ms. Tolbert particularly liked seminar-styled courses. Although Moorhead State University permitted students to take electives at the senior undergraduate level and graduate course in other departments, she found that the undergraduate courses were usually structured as lecture classes rather than as seminars, and that the other graduate courses were "beyond the generalist." She did take an Italian Renaissance Art course outside the program's own offerings and had to do a great deal of reading to become familiar with the terminology, but her reaction was "It was great!"

Instead of a final project, she was involved in writing three essays. One was on different philosophical approaches to overpopulation; one on patient-doctor trust relationships; one on Picasso's revolt against traditionalism. Her first paper she describes as being on a subject that is an ongoing interest for her; the second "relates to ethical consideration in the medical field (my work); the third is reaching out to understand modern art . . . [related to] our study of the idea of progress." The three-pronged approach allowed Ms. Talbot to satisfy an interest she had before entering the program; to complete a project that was an integral part of her work experience; and to explore a subject that emanated from the core course work of the program.

While certain goals are clearly defined by the student on entry, some do not emerge until the student is immersed in the program. One student in her early fifties at Moorhead State University had no vocational goals on entry. She claimed that she has "since been hired by a private college to teach freshman English on the basis of [her] degree." This ability to find new directions, although not initially sought, occurred in at least twenty-five percent of the cases reviewed.

Student Response To The Curriculum

One of the questions asked in the survey of students was: "Which courses did you particularly enjoy?" The following is a list of those mentioned: "Literature and History of the Vietnam War Era"; "The Oral Tradition"; "The Physiology of Positive Aging"; "Men and Work"; "The Age of Jackson"; "France from World War II to the Present"; "Renaissance Art"; "Technology, Bureaucracy and Identity in Modern America"; "The Western Idea of Progress"; "Human Sexuality and Gender Identity"; "The Moral Dimensions of Life"; "Western and Asian Expression"; "Energy and the Environment"; "The Marxist World View"; "Classical Roots of Modern Culture"; "Musical Experience: Reflections in Sound"; "Cross-cultural Study of Disease"; "Imagination, Reform, and the Urban Transformation"; "Literature and the Visual Arts"; "Comparative Political Institutions"; "The Self in Literature"; "The Mythic Frontier in American Culture"; "Modern Drama";

"Science and the Humanities"; "Mysticism, East and West"; "Women and Creativity"; "Arts and Ideas of the Twentieth Century"; "Job: When Bad Things Happen to Good People"; "Existentialism"; "Ecology"; "Genetics."

Many of the above courses clearly deal with value systems. At Georgetown University, Dr. Phyllis O'Callaghan, director of the Master of Arts in Liberal Studies program, reported in her article, "Teaching Values for Adults: Graduate Programs in Liberal Studies," that "each student is required to enroll in two human values courses. These courses directly address such questions of human value as moral growth, human freedom, comparative values in major world religions, theories of justice, the nature of human purpose, and personal and professional ethical questions."[6]

Most institutions include courses, either core or elective, that cover the gamut of questions mentioned above. Whereas more traditional programs might focus on the formal structural elements of their disciplines or on specialization of a single subject, values are the central orientation for these "non-traditional" interdisciplinary programs. The ability to synthesize materials from diverse disciplines is also a crucial objective of these Graduate Liberal Studies programs.

Although students took courses in a number of different areas, they found coherence in the programming through the establishment of connections that either they discovered from their own research or were indicated by the faculty who linked the electives to the core course content. A reflective essay drawing various threads together thematically is an exercise required in many of the programs and evoked the most enthusiastic student responses.

The Impact Of The Liberal Studies Program On Its Students

Administrators and students frequently ask what happens to graduates of Graduate Liberal Studies programs, since the degree is often described by the unfortunate epithet "terminal." Since this degree is not intended to train or prepare students for further graduate or professional degrees, or for explicit careers, although the latter may occur as an indirect result, it is difficult for most colleges to assess the benefits materially, as for example in job placement. However, the benefits that accrue to the students are more intangible and frequently relate more to their sense of well-being, self-confidence, and intellectual and spiritual awareness.

Following is a list of statements students provided regarding their view of the positive developments resulting from their study in these programs.

1. "I am a different person, having much expanded my intellectual horizons, interests and activities as well as my circle of friends. I am enthusiastic about eventually earning a Ph.D. . . . ."

2. "I enjoyed the excitement of learning and studying; discussing books and ideas with others in a disciplined environment."

3. "The course work has introduced me to new information, ideas and interesting people. The course requirements have forced me to polish up long-forgotten writing skills and to integrate knowledge and analyze major issues and problems."

4. "I find that I read much more and read more critically. My writing ability has also improved greatly."

5. "My primary benefit is a broader and more enriched view of my own situation in life and of reality in general. In addition, my greatly improved writing skills have increased my self-confidence."

6. "I have acquired a new way of looking at some complex problems, a way that can be applied to a variety of subjects."

7. "I have gained knowledge in diverse areas and have zeroed in on what I really want to do with the rest of my life."

8. "I am more knowledgeable; I have stretched my mind and renewed my teaching certificate as a result of this experience. I have also formed a very close friendship with another student in the program."

9. "The MLA program provides me with the opportunity to engage in new intellectual concerns and be with the kind of people that I do not usually meet through my work. It is very good therapy for me."[8]

111

10. "Increasingly, a police officer [sergeant] must have a broad knowledge in a number of academic areas because an officer's duties and responsibility are so complex. I believe that I can best fulfill this requirement through the pursuit of a graduate degree in the liberal arts. Not surprisingly, I have been able to apply a great deal of what I have learned to my job."[9]

11. "In the 'high tech' world we live in there seemed to be no way for a mature person like me, who loved the humanities, to pursue the liberal arts past the under-graduate level, in an academic setting. The M.A.L.S. program offered me just such an opportunity. The past four years have exposed me to art, literature, poetry, and the sciences in a way I could not have or *would not* have pursued on my own. The fact that the other students in my class were mostly over thirty, working or retired persons who felt a similar drive to acquire mastery in the liberal arts made the program doubly appealing."[10]

At times, graduates are able to fuse their personal development with concrete career and civic objectives. One such case is that of Margaret McNamara, a woman over sixty, who began her undergraduate studies in the Special Baccalaureate Degree Program for Adults at Brooklyn College of the City University of New York when she was in her fifties. After a long background as a purser on ships travelling to the Caribbean and to several countries on the East Coast of South America, she decided to pursue a Bachelor of Arts degree with a concentration in Latin American Studies. While she was yet an undergraduate, she was employed as a manager of publications for A.T.&T. She enrolled in the Master of Arts in Liberal Studies program at Brooklyn College in 1983 and was awarded a Fulbright Fellowship in the Fall of 1984 to study in Uruguay. A.T.&T. gave her a leave of absence to complete the project she undertook, "Energy in Uruguay: Background and Prospects." Professor Jose Luis Duomarco of the Department of Physics at the School of Engineering of the University of the Republic (Uruguay) served as one of her two thesis advisers. His field was solar energy. Ms. McNamara was awarded her degree in June, 1985, and was admitted to the doctoral program in history at the Graduate Center of the City University of New York, where she plans to continue her

112

studies in Latin America. The latter accomplishment had not been a consideration at the time of her entry to the Master's program; rather it was the consequence of her success in the program that motivated her continued learning.

Another case was reported in a local newspaper in Shreveport, Louisiana. On April 12, 1985, the Shreveport-Bossier *Times* wrote of the achievement of the first MLA graduate from the Louisiana State University at Shreveport. Twenty-five years earlier, Glenda Cooper had earned her degree in secondary education at LSU. A forty-three-year-old homemaker, she decided to take courses at LSU, and when the Graduate Liberal Studies program was initiated in 1984, she enrolled. She wanted to compete, wrote the *Times*, on an educational level with her husband, a physician, whom she had met as an undergraduate. "Her interest in communications led her to do the master's thesis on [the role of] public radio. She began by volunteering at KDAQ, the public radio station that began broadcasting [in 1984] from LSU."

Both Ms. McNamara and Ms. Cooper went on to accomplish more than they had foreseen on entry to the Graduate Liberal Studies program. For most students in these programs, as for the latter two individuals, an increase in self-confidence is a concomitant result of their participation in the program, and many are enabled to pursue new vocational or avocational interests.

Of course, many students enter these programs having already accomplished major professional goals. They are interested in new ventures in learning and relaxation. An eighteen-year-old undergraduate would not be as likely to say what Dr. Woody Wilson, an internist and a student at Louisiana State University's MLA program, said, "It's very relaxing when you are worrying about Dante's *Inferno* and not about other people's problems."[11]

Ms. Cooper voiced the sentiments of many adults when she said that her appreciation of the liberal arts subjects was greater now than it would have been years ago and added, "People should realize [that] education is becoming a lifelong process. You never have to stop."[12] Ms. Cooper's attitude, if generalized to the adult population in the next decade, as so many educators are predicting, means more adults will be seeking new learning experiences.

The Prognosis For Future Enrollments

One of the concerns of administrators contemplating the establishment of a new Graduate Liberal Studies program or deciding whether to continue support of an existing program is future enrollment. Long-range planning involves assessing both demographic and curricular trends.

A major trend that will affect enrollment is the increasing tendency of individuals to drop in and out of formal learning situations.[13] The notion that after one has obtained a degree in a traditional age group, one has completed formal academic learning no longer holds true. Not only have former drop-outs and older adults returned for an undergraduate education, but more are also pursuing advanced studies. While some are seeking a general education, some are also interested in teaching credentials or advanced degrees for middle management positions. Many Graduate Liberal Studies programs satisfy these multiple objectives.

Equal opportunity programs have also enabled minorities and women to avail themselves of an undergraduate education.[14] While minority participation is generally low in adult education, the 1981 census of Americans over the age of eighteen found that thirteen percent of all Hispanics and black adults were participating in part-time adult education and training, and of these fifteen percent were enrolled in some kind of course work, largely at the undergraduate level. As more minorities are appointed to middle management positions, primarily in human resources areas, more might be attracted to the kind of values-oriented curriculum that constitutes Graduate Liberal Studies programs. Even now, sixty percent of the students enrolled in Graduate Liberal Studies programs hold middle management positions. Women are already dominant in these programs, and this trend is likely to continue.

With the baby boom generation heading into their fifties in the next decade, the number of adults seeking a new learning experience should increase sharply, for, as K. Patricia Cross points out, with increased use of leisure time, more adults seek learning experiences.[15]

Of course, not all research is encouraging in regard to enrollment in graduate programs that are not job-related. Kathryn Mohrman, in "Adult Students and the Humanities,"[16] states that humanities courses represented only seven-and-seven-tenths percent of the total courses adults enrolled in during 1981; only four tenths of a percent were at the graduate level and only two percent of the adult population were enrolled out of the thirteen percent engaged in any kind of part-time learning. Mohrman's data do not address the entire picture for Graduate Liberal Studies programs since the curriculum bridges the humanities, social sciences, and sciences. As interest in job-related goals drops off after the age of fifty, more of this age group could be attracted to Graduate Liberal Studies programs. Studies show that about two thirds of adult learners want some kind of recognition for their learning, and a degree program has such an appeal.

Studies indicate that adults in their forties and fifties may work at a slower pace than those in their twenties and thirties.[17] Graduate Liberal Studies programs, based less on acquisition of many facts and more on analysis of smaller doses of information, are therefore better suited to this older adult group.

Cross's description of an ideal curriculum for adults, one that emphasizes "the development of cognitive functions calling for integration, interpretation and application of knowledge," is the strongest recommendation to date for the liberal studies model.[18]

It is clear that the pool of adult learners ready for graduate-level studies will increase over the next decade, and that a curriculum that can prove that it is built on the strengths and needs of an older adult population will have the greatest attraction.

The flexibility of time-frame and curricular design, the focus on human values and ethical concerns, the attention to synthesis as well as analysis are all positive features that indicate the readiness of Graduate Liberal Studies programs to meet the growing needs of a larger and more mature adult population.

Barbara L. Gerber, Ph.D.
Brooklyn College

1. A number of the programs are organized, however, in terms of concentrations such as American Studies; International Studies; Landmarks in Western Thought; Women's Studies; Translation; or Museum Studies. Most define liberal studies in terms of disciplines usually associated with the Humanities or Social Sciences, but a sizable number also includes the Natural Sciences under this rubric. Only a few include technology in their definition of liberal studies, and when they do offer courses, they present them as technology and society rather than as courses describing technologies.

2. The instruments used in order to respond to these questions were the following: a questionnaire distributed to the directors of Master of Arts in Liberal Studies Programs affiliated with the Association of Graduate Liberal Studies Programs (AGLSP, now located at Georgetown University, Washington, D.C., under the direction of Dr. Phyllis O'Callaghan); the fact sheets included in the AGLSP Portfolio; brochures and bulletins of the colleges and universities offering such programs; self-studies of a number of these institutions, including those of Brooklyn College of the City University of New York; Texas Christian University; De Paul University; and Duke University; a questionnaire submitted to both students currently enrolled and graduates at representative institutions in various regions of the country, including Baker University, Brooklyn College, De Paul University, The Johns Hopkins University, Dartmouth College, Moorhead State University, and Xavier University. The names of the students were given by the directors of their respective programs.

3. Daniel Fallon, "The New Master's Degrees," in *Change*, 20 (October, 1978), pp. 19-22.

4. (San Francisco: Jossey-Bass Publishers, 1981), pp. 68-69. Her observations are based on Solmon, Gordon, and Ocsner's study in 1979, using data from the Cooperative Institutional Research Program (CIRP), updating Homstrom's 1973 analysis. Their analysis covered 172,400

adults over the age of 21 who entered college between 1966 and 1978.

5. The profiles of Mr. Dorman, Mr. Knowlton, Mr. Reichert and Ms. Tolbert as well as all the references to students in this segment are based on the questionnaire responses they submitted in the spring of 1986.

6. Dr. O'Callaghan is currently the president of the Association of Graduate Liberal Studies Programs. This chapter is in *Teaching Values and Ethics in College, New Directions for Teaching and Learning*, ed. by M. J. Collins. No. 13, 48 (San Francisco: Jossey-Bass, March, 1983), pp. 45-52.

7. Responses 1 through 8 are derived from the questionnaire submitted to students from 17 MLA programs.

8. Moorhead State University MLA brochure; this statement was attributed to Mr. Samuel Wai, a budget administrator for American Crystal Sugar.

9. *Ibid.* This statement was attributed to Mr. John Wagner, a sergeant with the Fergus Falls Police Department in Minnesota.

10. Letter dated June 9, 1986, addressed to the director of the Brooklyn College MLA program.

11. The Shreveport *Times*, May 13, 1984.

12. The Shreveport *Times*, April 12, 1985.

13. Cross, p. 68.

14. Cross, p. 68.

15. Cross, p. 95.

16. (Washington, D.C. : Association of American Colleges, 1981), Table 1 and p. 3.

17. Cross, p. 155, citing A. B. Knox, *Adult Development and Learning: A Handbook on Individual Growth and Competence in the Adult Years for Education and the*

Helping Professions (San Francisco: Jossey-Bass, 1977), p. 422.

18. Cross, p. 163.

THREE GRADUATES SPEAK

———

REACHING

My experience as a student in a Graduate Liberal Studies program has meant a great deal to me in a great many ways. Perhaps I can best organize my reactions to the program by suggesting how it has affected me philosophically, professionally, and personally, though even this approach is difficult, because these three areas are integrated in my life just as they are in a Graduate Liberal Studies program. As a person always interested in learning more myself, as well as in educating others (I've been a public school teacher for more than thirty years), I am convinced that American education today needs to place much greater emphasis than it does on liberal studies. There has been so much emphasis in the last several decades upon science and technology, acceleration, practical skills and job education that we have been producing generations of specialists who may be "successful" in their occupations but are often miserable in their lives. We keep hearing, too, about the relativity of values. Educated, we often discard our inherited value system, in whole or in part, yet are left with little to take its place.

As a senior high school teacher, I have become increasingly concerned about the tendency toward fragmentation in modern education. In most secondary schools the day is scheduled into separate little blocks of learning: fifty minutes of social studies, fifty minutes of math, fifty minutes of English, and so on and so on in a neatly compartmentalized seven-period day. Seldom is there any provision for teachers of different subject areas to come together to share information and ideas. Even more lamentable is the fact that students themselves are subjected to this departmentalization of learning; specifics of separate subjects are poured into their minds, but little (or often no) effort is made to demonstrate the interrelationship of the separate offerings.

There is no opportunity for synthesis, no continuity, no discussion of the "why." We send students off into the world prepared with smatterings of learning in different areas, but unprepared for life.

I was more fortunate than many. Even before I left high school my family had decided that I would attend a small, private, liberal arts college. As an adventurous young soul eager to be off on her own, attending a small Catholic women's college in the same city where I had spent all my life was certainly not my idea of what college should be. I found, however, that that college (Trinity in Washington, D.C.) was just what a college should be. As a student there in the early fifties, I was required to take--along with some fifty-four credit hours of my English major--courses in philosophy, theology, history, science, and foreign language. Though I complained at the time, I have since come to believe that those forty or more credit-hours of philosophy and theology have contributed as much to my success as a teacher as have the courses in my major. College, then, was not just learning; it was the opening up of whole new worlds of ideas to me. It was indeed a full and rich preparation for life.

I graduated, taught English in a junior high school, and, in the late fifties, somehow found time along with marriage and childbearing to earn a Master of Arts degree in English. That was the end of specialization. For the next twenty years I was free (as time allowed) to explore those other subjects of considerable interest to me--particularly the arts and philosophy. As a teacher of English, I found much wealth in these areas to enrich my teaching.

In the late sixties I became very interested in a humanities approach to teaching. "Humanities," of course, means different things to different people. To me it was an answer to the fragmentation so prevalent in secondary schools. So much was this true that, although I had not desired to be anything but a classroom teacher, I was persuaded to apply for a position in a newly funded Title III, ESEA project. I liked the sound of its emphasis upon the humanities, its encouragement of creativity, and its utilization of community resource places and persons. As an assistant director of the Title III project, I worked with teachers of art, music, social studies, and English to encourage interdisciplinary approaches to education.

Several years after I returned to the classroom I was selected to teach at the newly formed high school for the arts, now the Duke Ellington School of the Arts, where the students are given an opportunity for specialized training in an arts major along with a full academic program. It was exciting to be in an arts-centered environment. I think I grew with the school, never sacrificing the grammar, composition, and literature, which I knew to be so important, but enriching that teaching with what I knew of the arts and what I continued to learn both from my associates and on my own. I felt fairly good about what I was doing--just little things like using examples from the Hudson River School to enrich my teaching of Romanticism in American literature or slides from the National Gallery of Art in association with my teaching of mythology. But I really needed to learn more about the subjects I kept talking about.

When I first learned about the Graduate Liberal Studies program at Georgetown University, I laughed at myself for considering a return to school. I had more than met all the academic requirements for my career and had no desire to move into a different position. Besides, with a growing family, I had more than enough to keep me busy. But I read the list of offerings and stopped laughing. There were music, art, philosophy, history, and literature courses--and they all blended with one another! I couldn't resist.

It was with trepidation, though, that I took my first step. Would I be laughed at, I wondered--an older woman playing the role of a neophyte scholar? Perhaps not; the Graduate Liberal Studies program at Georgetown was part of the Division of Continuing Education. Would I still be able to learn? My brain was two decades older than when I had last gone to school. Would I be a disgrace to my profession, a teacher no longer capable of being a successful student? Having worked for years teaching young people how to write an essay, would I myself be able to write one?

I decided to play it safe. I began with literature courses--and in a short time I managed to learn a great deal about the subject I had been teaching for years. Later I made it through "Nineteenth Century Painting," and was brave enough to tackle--very successfully, as it turned out-- "Images of Authority in African Art." And then came the course that made so much difference in my thinking and in my teaching. I needed to meet the requirement of taking one of the "Core" values courses. I didn't want any that dealt with self-analysis (very dangerous stuff in my opinion), nor did I want "Death and Dying" (which I was not yet ready to deal with). That left only one--"Comparative Values and International Relations." I was skeptical, but what else was there? As it turned out, the instructor, a Jesuit rich in age and wisdom, was one of the most inspiring teachers I have ever known. He had lived with the people about whom he spoke. When he taught Hinduism or Buddhism, Shintoism or Islam, there was no "us" or "them." We, his students, learned to think in new/old ways and to see the universality in diversity. "We cannot hope for peace in the world," he would say, "until our young people are taught to understand how others think and what they believe."

When it came time for me to choose a subject for my final project there was no doubt about what I would do--I had to follow, in my small way, his suggestion. The inspiration had been given; there was only the work to be done. After a year of organizing notes and doing additional research I had what I wanted--not only my final project/thesis, but a detailed outline of a course which I called "Comparative Values and the Arts," a course which I later began to teach to my high school students and one which I still love teaching.

My study of other cultures has also enriched my teaching of mythology to my ninth graders. As texts became more accessible in the seventies, I had supplemented my teaching of traditional Greek and Roman mythology with a few Native American and African myths. Now I began to search for texts with Asian and Pacific mythology to add to my curriculum. There were none, so I applied for a Council for Basic Education/N.E.H. grant for the summer of 1983 to develop my own anthology. Surprise! I received one of their awards for Independent Study in the Humanities, and I suddenly found myself deep in research, writing a book, when some five years before I had doubted my ability even to become a student again.

Of all the marvelous old stories of the past, one of my favorites is the myth of Prometheus and his brother Epimetheus. Epimetheus, he who acted first and thought later, created animals, giving them acute senses, protective covering, and an instinctive perception of the dangerous. All these special gifts having been given to the beasts, there was little left for Prometheus to bestow upon the naked, short-sighted, weak creature called man. But Prometheus, he who thought before he acted, was able to conceive something special as a gift for humankind--a mind: the capacity to reason, to imagine, to dream. He set the creature upon two legs, not four, so that it could look upward. With its hands and mind and soul, it could reach.

It is that ability and audacity to keep reaching which, I think, makes us truly human. When it is stripped from us, we have little else to lose. Just as one breathes deeply, stretches the arms and legs, raises the shoulders and chest, conditioning the body for rigorous physical exercise, so one needs to continue to stretch the mind, the soul--to reach as far out and as far upward as possible. This, to me, is what a Graduate Liberal Studies program is all about. It is a reaching far out into other disciplines, other approaches, other concepts, other people.

It is also a special personal experience. There are different points in one's life when one is tempted to reach no longer. One finds at suburban cocktail parties and on city streets those who have ceased to reach. And I, too, am at that time of life when one is thus tempted--those autumn years when one's children are grown, one's home nearly paid for but now much in need of repair, one's body tiring, one's face lined with the heat and dryness of past years. Life is easier now as far as material things are concerned. We are past the years, so romantic and wonderful in memory, when we wondered when the next baby would come and where the next meal would come from.

Yet, in other ways, it is not so easy. In the turmoil of earlier years there was something special which kept us going; there was always something to work for, to look forward to--there were dreams. Some of these dreams may have come true, others not. It does not matter much now. What truly matters, I think, is having the audacity to continue to dream--to keep reaching. There must be something to work for, to look forward to, so that one does not find oneself always fretting about what may go wrong with one's health or one's home--or about what has gone wrong already.

My Graduate Liberal Studies program helped me to keep reaching. And, as I looked around the classroom and shared ideas with fellow students of all different backgrounds and ages, I sensed that this was true for them also. What will I do now that I have nearly completed the work for an Advanced Certificate in Liberal Studies? I think I'll still keep taking classes. I know I'll continue to work in the school where I teach students to integrate learning experiences. I'll do what I can in that regard in the school system

123

too. Maybe when I retire from the public schools, I'll start my own school, a high school based on a liberal studies curriculum. Where do I go from here? I don't know. But I do know that the important thing is that I still have the capacity and the audacity to keep reaching, reaching out and reaching up.

Ann Coluzzi
Graduate, Georgetown University

THE "FIT" OF COURSES

It probably seems strange that the idea of pursuing and attaining a Master of Arts in Humanities degree surfaced and was decided within an instant. But so it was with me. One morning, over coffee, I read an article in the newspaper about such a program being initiated by Xavier University in Cincinnati. It would be taught by teams of the University's outstanding professors. It would be taught at night, with a four-course requirement focusing on the topic of heroes, one course per semester for two years. The balance of courses would be chosen by students with the approval of faculty. I enrolled that morning. The program spoke with great immediacy to my long-dormant longing to learn in a structured environment, to discuss ideas for their own sake, to set foot in some new fields of knowledge, to test myself in the rigor of an academic discipline, and to enter a new setting, in this case, a Jesuit University.

I am a married woman with grown children and a job which is practical and action-oriented. On behalf of the Cincinnati Business Committee and the Greater Cincinnati Chamber of Commerce, I develop and manage programs involving cooperation between the business community on the one hand and the Cincinnati Public Schools and the Archdiocese of Cincinnati on the other. I work with the people who make the city and the schools "work": teachers, administrators, students, politicians, business executives, university officials, and leaders of various civic, ethnic, and religious groups. I enjoy the wide variety of people I meet;

enjoy both continuity and flux; enjoy finding new ways to ameliorate or solve problems, particularly in the schools. Cincinnati is, in my opinion, a leader in making schools more effective through community involvement. Innovative and creative efforts move quickly from planning to implementation here. My work life is full and fascinating.

But the Graduate Liberal Studies program struck me as being too good to pass up. One immediate value was that it would give me some personal balance. The program would be contemplative in contrast with the practical activity of my work. It would permit me to step into a scholarly mode. I could relish, savor, debate, and grow from ideas organized for study by experienced professors who themselves were attracted to interdisciplinary studies. I would have the opportunity to take advantage of a college atmosphere as an adult, not as the girl I was during my undergraduate years, and to filter whatever knowledge came my way through the indeterminate experience and wisdom that my years (forty-seven at the time) provided.

A high value was the opportunity to synthesize and connect fragments of knowledge: the interdisciplinary approach itself. Compartmentalizing in disciplines, units, departments or bureaucracies has its uses. But pieces are rarely united into wholes. A whole never becomes the sum of its parts; once we start to live with the parts, it may well be that re-assembling is beyond us! Specialized language, or jargon if it is not one's own, separates us further, and we tend to narrow our focus as we become more experienced in our own niches. Studying in an organized curriculum with professors and students looking at ideas together from a diversity of backgrounds, chronological ages and perspectives promised to be, and was, of inestimable value.

I now had a chance to learn something about areas in which I was ignorant. The program did not, as it could not, fill all those enormous gaps in my knowledge. It did, as I had hoped, shine some light into some of my dark spaces. It especially gave me insight into Eastern thinking and cultures, into music, and into scientific processes in biology and physics. Cincinnati is a medium-sized city, yet now that I am attuned to and interested in a wide spectrum of ideas, I find that it is rich in resources for anything I want to pursue, culturally or intellectually. Until I got into the Graduate Liberal Studies program, however, I was unaware of these resources and their accessibility, and of how warmly people in charge of the resources would respond to the most uninformed questions.

Another value of the program was the wonderful feeling of freedom I got from the pursuit of knowledge for its own sake. Many classmates felt somewhat sheepish to be enrolled in a program that was not aimed at career improvement. That was not my feeling at all. For those who feel a need to be defensive on that score I would argue in hindsight that the program can readily be defended on the ground that it has strong practical merit. Yet, because of the sense of freedom which I valued, and because the need to obtain the degree was entirely internal, I severely disciplined myself to place a high priority on attendance, on completing the reading and written work, and on meeting the timeline I had artificially set (one night school course per semester for five years). I knew that circumstances in my job, in job-related travel, family, and volunteer obligations would surely intervene, and they did. At times it took single-minded purpose and near despair to slog ahead. It was worth it. The freedom to take whatever I chose (within the humanities limits) and the discipline I exerted when the pressure from other events was strong gave added value to the attainment of this degree.

I received still other values during my five-year extended wandering, which fittingly began with a study of Odysseus. Discovering ways of thinking that had been unknown to me has broadened my perspective, given me helpful tools, and altered my ways of approaching nearly everything I do. It confirmed and increased my confidence in many approaches which I had taken intuitively rather than thoughtfully. First, with the helpful direction set by the study of heroes in the required initial courses, I have been alert to leadership well beyond classic heroes. In an important way, the study of heroes as a leitmotif has helped me to be, in my jargon, a "community builder." Second, as a goal-oriented, future-directed American, some exposure to the mystical concepts of a timeless spaceless now; to a sense of balance in contrast to an ideal of linear improvement; to a respect for emotion, intuition and sensation as well as for logic and reason has been of boundless value. Third, getting to know faculty members and university life, brushing up on the research resources in the city, and meeting another cross-section of people in the city were refreshing. My becoming a student was role-reversal for my children, who were all fairly recent college graduates. All three gave me encouragement and savvy tips. The ages of students in my classes ranged from twenty to over seventy; attitudes shaped by age were interesting. One night the knowledgeable teacher of philosophy remarked that 1952 was a memorable year in his life (as well as in the the life of the author being discussed): he had been born in 1952. My mind, too, remembered 1952: it was the year my husband and I had been married. Class discussion encompassed several perspectives about that year.

Ruminating over classical heroes, self-effacing mystics, explorers, discoverers, despots, and "movers and shakers" in the civic and business world has influenced not only my studies but my work as well. As I ponder the role an individual can play here and now, it is beneficial for me to be more immediately aware of a vast array of possible human actions. Whether or not the connotation of "hero" is appropriate, there is, in today's cities, ample room for, and examples of, individuals who make a constructive difference. About four years ago I came across a quotation (attribution unknown to me) that succinctly spoke to my current thinking: "A good leader is one who inspires his followers with confidence in him. A great leader is one who inspires his followers with confidence in themselves."

In my reading on Taoism, the same idea was expressed more poetically and quite vividly by Lao Tzu in the seventh century B.C. :

A leader is best
When people barely know that he exists,
Not so good when people obey and acclaim him,
Worst when they despise him.
"Fail to honor people,
They fail to honor you,"
But of a good leader, who talks little,
When his work is done, his aim fulfilled,
They will all say, "We did this ourselves."

The role of leadership and its relationship to the building of a healthy community is something which I will continue to think about; it is of crucial import to the life of a city and the schooling of children. My study of the humanities has given my thinking a framework.

The messages of religions and philosophical mysticism delivered through the centuries had been completely unexamined by me. I continue to learn more about Eastern cultures on my own and to notice the connectedness of all.

Reading the same concepts in the words of respected physicists, Eastern sages, and American and English authors has made me more comfortable with ideas which, when I had heard them previously, were couched in terms which were alien to me: "ineffable," "left or right brained," "What is the sound of one hand clapping?" However, it was a course on mysticism that opened me (and my still-small fund of understanding at least permits me to be aware that the course opened me, and not just my mind) to a remarkable and rich way of exploring life. Given a proclivity toward interdisciplinary studies, I find that further exploration of the unity of all things now seems a natural direction to follow. In a practical sense, by learning to be comfortable with paradox, something more compatible with Eastern than Western thought, I have learned to be more balanced in my understanding of the similarities and diversities among people in the city.

The interdisciplinary mode certainly made me see linkages between courses, even when those linkages had not been consciously planned. I chose from a fairly small selection of courses offered at night within the disciplines approved for the degree. Linkages may have been divine intervention, part of a cosmic plan, serendipity, blind coincidence, or simply my own inference. Still, the study of each course seemed to provide information that helped to make the next course more meaningful for me.

One course examined Darwin and Marx from the different perspectives of biology and philosophy. Professors and students were equally off-balance. Those comfortable in the arts were not comfortable in the sciences, and vice versa; all were on slippery territory. Paradoxically people seemed freer to speak about their tentative ideas and to reveal their preconceived, frequently erroneous notions. That course, like others where professors were first exposed to other disciplines, was filled with the excitement, truly palpable, of fresh insight. In that course, for example, I "discovered" Marx's view of economics; previously I had known only a little about his theory of communism. His analysis of the past made a great deal of sense to me, particularly his thesis that economic change occurred when the tools for change were in place. In his time major legal, social, and religious changes had to occur in order to establish a new status quo which fit the changed economic conditions. I tried to apply his ideas to the next course I took--a course in which the English Reformation was presented to us as a religious reformation. With the powerful zeal of a student with a half-baked, firmly-held notion, I rejected that thesis. I put enormous energy and time into trying to prove that the English Reformation was an economic revolution, and that the religious change was simply a necessary side effect. I think that I was the only one who heard that particular drumbeat, but it was an exhilarating experience to be so emotionally involved in "counting the number of angels on the head of a pin" and enjoying it so much. Certainly I learned a great deal.

The synthesizing continued right to the end. My study of ancient heroes and, in another course, my study of Kant helped to focus my final paper. I felt the need to circle back to the beginning of the program and write about King Arthur, examining the perspectives of three authors who wrote their versions of the Arthurian legend: Alfred Lord Tennyson, T. H. White, and Thomas Berger. Tennyson was particularly appealing to me because I found his characters and his vision of Camelot strongly imbued with Kantian philosophy and ideals. Thus once again I had the opportunity to try to integrate knowledge I had received from two different, and apparently unrelated, sources.

My experience with a Graduate Liberal Studies program convinced me that interdisciplinary programs at all levels of education are sorely needed. The curriculum of a Graduate Liberal Studies program not only provides an opportunity to dip into many disciplines within the humanities but also provokes discovery and connections across the disciplines. My participation, and growth, in the program will benefit my future as well as my present.

I believe there is an intuitive understanding "out there" that interdisciplinary studies, connectedness between people and ideas, are important today. The world is growing demonstrably smaller; it is also expanding exponentially. Interdisciplinary studies make good sense; they are logical; they work intellectually, intuitively, and emotionally. They need to be made a part of the mainstream of academic studies at the university level, and perhaps at primary and secondary levels as well. The need for interdisciplinary thinking is a need for all of society, not academia alone. Perhaps there is a role for others beyond university walls to play in broadening the base of support for interdisciplinary programs.

Carol L. Davidow
Graduate, Xavier University

A GUEST WHO DID NOT KNOW HERSELF TOO LATE

I came to a Graduate Liberal Studies program after spending many years as an executive secretary in jobs that required practical skills, good judgment, and common sense, but were, from an intellectual standpoint, barren of challenge. I had graduated from college in the 1940's, and like many bright southern girls at the time, had gone there because it had seemed an interesting thing to do if one wasn't ready to get married. I tried majoring in Art and then in English (I couldn't decide between them), but, although I was elected to Phi Beta Kappa, I never considered getting an advanced degree, nor had I prepared for a career. Either would have been unusual for a girl at that time and place, unless perhaps she wanted to teach. So after college I drifted into secretarial work and eventually moved to New York. Since I usually worked in professional rather than business organizations, many of my bosses had doctoral degrees, but it never occurred to me that I might be able to do serious graduate work, although I was often told that I was "overqualified" for my jobs. For one thing, I thought that one should have a very specific career goal in mind before even considering such a thing. Yet I had always been "bookish." As a child I used to read the encyclopedia for fun, and even before I could write I made up little "poems." In fact the world recreated through language always seemed as interesting to me as the world of people and objects around me.

As an adult, I partly assuaged the nagging feeling that I was neglecting both my interests and talents by occasionally taking "continuing education" courses in art, art history, and poetry. These were pleasant and non-threatening, since they involved no exams, papers or grades, but they offered little challenge. Not until I was almost fifty years old did I finally decide, for some reason, to take a course--Modern British Literature--for credit. Well, it was a revelation to discover that I could still study, absorb information, pass an examination, write a paper, and get an A. Okay, I thought, even at this late date, maybe I could still go to graduate

130

school--if only to see what would happen. This idea, frankly, scared me, and it was a while before I followed through. As each semester rolled around, I would again sign up for another "general studies" course at the New School of Social Research in New York City; I took writing, philosophy, even a literature course that questioned the value of studying literature. One day I was doing minor chores around the apartment and listening to one of those "talking heads" programs. Mortimer Adler was making some philosophical point, and as I became aware of how interested I was in this fairly heavy discussion, a question seemed to rise up inside of me: "I wonder if it *is* too late to live the life of the mind?" I knew that for me graduate school was the only way I could answer this question. I knew from experience that reading on my own, in isolation, without guidance or feedback from like-minded people just didn't give me the stimulation or direction I needed. But still I hesitated and rationalized: why jump in when I didn't even know what subject I wanted to study?

At this point I read about the Master of Arts in Liberal Studies program at the New School, and it seemed exactly the program for someone like me. The course offerings were broad and various, and, better, I would not be required (as I would be in traditional programs) to eliminate certain areas of interest in order to become expert in a single area. It even seemed that not yet having made up my mind on the one thing that *really* interested me might be an advantage rather than a disadvantage! Such freedom was just what I wanted at that point--the freedom to have the chance to learn more and more about more and more. Looking back, my aspirations seemed a bit over-ambitious, especially at that point in my life, yet in the Graduate Liberal Studies program I found an approach to graduate study that understood my needs and gave encouragement to students like me who wanted to acquire greater knowledge in many areas. Moreover the program had a rationale for the variety of courses it offered, and a coherent plan that emphasized the relationships between literature, history, philosophy, sociology, and art. Thus it had what ordinary adult education programs did not have--a structure and a goal. The structure was not a cut-and-dried series of required courses but a framework around which to create one's own original pattern of study, and perhaps even discover an internal coherence in one's own particular interests. I could also sense, after a very short time, that the directors of the program not only

131

tolerated older students (because of the law) but actually desired them.

Although I was still working full-time, I enrolled in two courses the first semester--one that related visual art to psychological theory and one on the tragic drama. I found their content to be very rich, the classes small enough for the students to be seen as individuals, and the teachers to be enthusiastic. So it was with all subsequent courses: the teachers not only seemed to like teaching but especially liked teaching the kind of students attracted to liberal studies at the graduate level--non-specialist students and students by choice, whose ages ranged from the early twenties to over sixty. Many of my fellow students were adults already established in careers--adults who obviously considered graduate study as a means of enhancing their lives rather than as preparation for higher-paying jobs. I immediately felt at home and, even better, felt that at last I was doing something that called on me to use my best abilities to the utmost. The program was certainly not a playground for dilettantes. There were requirements to be fulfilled, and a thesis or project to be completed. I found myself so interested in what I was studying that in addition to earning the required credits, I audited several courses. And although an auditor gets no grade and doesn't have to do a paper, I felt I had such a good idea for a paper in one of these courses--Mysticism and Modern Literature--that I had to write one. It was on Hart Crane's poem *The Bridge*, and I think it turned out to be one of my best.

Quite early in the program I realized that my concentration of studies was going to be in literature (apparently I just had to get my feet wet to know that), and it was a passage from *The Bridge* that influenced me to continue my studies after I earned a Master's degree. Contemplating his destiny as a poet whose "news" (or poetic themes) had been "already told" by greater poets, Crane writes:

So, must we from the hawk's far stemming view,
Must we descend as worm's eye to construe
Our love of all we touch, and take it to the Gate
As humbly as a guest who knows himself too late,
His news already told? Yes, while the heart is wrung,
Arise--yes, take this sheaf of dust upon your tongue!

As an older student, I also felt I was a "guest who knows himself too late," and as a literature student, I felt almost as much despair at the unlikelihood of having an original insight in writing about the literary canon as Crane did at the difficulty of original poetic creation. Just the same, my response to the prospect of attempting it was, like Crane's, "Yes."

Also quite early in the program, in a course on Aesthetics, another poem seemed to speak to my situation. In it Rilke recreates his encounter with a ruined and headless torso of Apollo. As he contemplates the statue, Rilke begins to feel that this fragment of stone is also contemplating him and, moreover, sending him a message-- "You must change your life." On reading the poem, I realized that, like the poet Rilke, I, too, had the faculty of responding to art as if to a living thing, and it seemed to me that the ancient Apollo (who is, after all, the god of poetry), through my response to the poem, had also spoken to me. And if I were to change, I realized that my worst mistake would come not from trying to be more than I could be, but in trying to be less.

So it is that since receiving the M.A.L.S. degree, I have gone on to do further graduate work in English at another university. So far, I have done well, in spite of the more impersonal atmosphere, more rigid requirements, competition for grades, and the inevitable tensions which these can arouse in a student. Most of my Graduate Liberal Studies courses were considered relevant and will count as credits toward the Ph.D. But what is much more important than the credits is that without the prior experience of success in the liberal studies program, with its emphasis on learning as its own reward and the freedom it allows for students to progress at their own pace, I wouldn't have had the courage to enter the more traditional advanced academic program I am in now. I don't yet know how far I can go--or how far I want to go. I do know, however, that what I gained from earning the Graduate Liberal Studies degree and what I learned from the additional studies it made possible are more than worth the time, money, and hard work they cost. In providing me with an environment to develop abilities that had lain unused for many years, the Graduate Liberal Studies program has given me a feeling of real achievement and the chance to point my life in a new direction.

Betty Coats Lindsey
Graduate, New School
for Social Research

133

GRADUATE LIBERAL STUDIES:
TRADITION AND EVOLUTION

Graduate Liberal Studies is alive and well. That is attested by the preceding essays in this volume, as well as by the many participants in programs throughout the country. Responses to a recent survey indicate that more than 7,000 students are currently enrolled in programs, and more than 18,000 students have graduated. The numbers would be even greater if all programs were included.

Taken together, these programs are affecting the lives of many thousands of mature adults who are enrolled in them. Most of the programs are found in private institutions, particularly liberal arts colleges, but a growing number of them are appearing in public and more diverse institutions. The national organization, the Association of Graduate Liberal Studies Programs, has grown to include nearly one hundred institutions, as well as other individuals concerned with the movement. Most institutions already conduct programs, while others are actively engaged in developing them. The Graduate Liberal Studies degree has become recognized by traditional organizations of graduate study as a new dimension of advanced education.

It is hard to imagine that this has happened in so short a time. The first program, at Wesleyan University, began barely more than thirty years ago in 1954. A few others followed in the 1960's and 1970's. Representatives of a dozen of these, graced with the hospitality of Dartmouth College, met in the woods of New Hampshire in 1975 to form the Association of Graduate Liberal Studies Programs. Members of that small band sought to encourage each other, to articulate a vision and a set of standards for the practice of liberal studies at the graduate level, and to assist others who wished to develop new programs. The real increase in the number of programs came in the late 1970's and 1980's, due in part to the Association's role as advocate and midwife, but even more to the increasing demand of an already well educated and curious adult population for organized, sustained study of areas of knowledge that would enrich their lives.

It is hard to apply the word "tradition" to such a short experience. Part of the answer to this paradox lies in the elegant essay by William Chace earlier in this volume. He alludes to King Lear's question about the "true need" of human existence. Surely, Lear says, we need more than the bare minimum of survival that all living organisms require. Chace concurs and suggests that in order to fulfill our humanity we need beauty, delight, and understanding. As he says, "the incremental, the extra, is what makes us interesting" and constitutes our retinue. And it is through study, reflection and enhancement of that treasure that humans take their existence beyond mere survival. We moderns have most commonly done that through liberal education, and liberal studies at the graduate level belong to the strong and deep tradition of liberal education.

The rest of the answer to why Graduate Liberal Studies can claim a tradition is that, despite its short life, it has already established a distinctive character that sets it apart from other forms of study. Graduate Liberal Studies is not traditional liberal education, although it is akin to it. It is not specialized graduate education, although it shares the same concern for high standards and advanced sophistication of understanding. It is not initiatory for young adults, but rather addresses and draws upon the maturity and experience of its participants. It is indeed its own animal.

This is not to gainsay the heterogeneity of programs that David House has described earlier. Variety is ensured by many different alternatives, deriving from the character of the host institutions, the particular visions of faculty, the mix of students who "select themselves" into the programs, and the inherent antinomianism of an intellectual effort that seeks to look at familiar texts, issues and topics from fresh perspectives. Much of the value of Graduate Liberal Studies lies in this pluralism.

At the same time there are several distinctive characteristics of Graduate Liberal Studies which are not usually found among other programs, whether they be graduate or undergraduate. I would single out four features: interdisciplinarity, distinctive curricular elements designed specifically for the programs, special orientations that reflect the particular nature of the institutions that sponsor them, and integrative or summative projects.

An interdisciplinary perspective has been the foundation stone of all the programs offered by members of the Association of Graduate Liberal Studies Programs. This interdisciplinarity has been achieved in many different ways. Some programs have provided team teaching by faculty from different disciplines who have worked around a common theme. Some have enriched the presentations of a single faculty member by bringing perspectives of other faculty to the class. Many creative faculty have left the mooring of their home disciplines to examine broad topics and issues from multiple vantage points. Some of the most fruitful experiences have occurred when wise and mature faculty have undertaken to explore major intellectual questions regardless of the confines of a single disciplinary orientation. Above all, what liberal studies faculty have sought to do is to consider questions in context and to see the connectedness of knowledge. This exploration is satisfying to students who as adults experience problems in their totality rather than as abstract and isolated phenomena. It is also satisfying to faculty who can pursue issues to a fuller understanding.

The various Graduate Liberal Studies programs also have special curricular elements that have been created specially to serve distinctive programmatic needs. Far from being hodgepodges of courses which already exist in the catalog, the well developed Graduate Liberal Studies program will be founded on uniquely designed content which illustrates and exemplifies the philosophy both of liberal studies and of the particular program of which it is a part. Frequently this distinction is manifested in a number of core courses that are either required of all students or from which students must select a certain number to form a foundation element of their study. It is through these core courses that students are made aware of the interdisciplinary, integrative character of liberal studies and in which they learn to re-examine assumptions they may have brought to the program. In other cases, special seminars may be designed to serve a similar purpose. In still others, students may be asked to undertake a special study or project under the direction of a faculty member and within guidelines set by the program. Whatever the particular curriculum design, its special elements seek to convey a liberal studies approach.

Similarly, programs usually describe their own unique traditions through a special character or theme that reflects the outlook of the host institution. This character may be deeply rooted in the mission of the institution or in an intellectual tradition which has grown up within the faculty. Such would be the case with the commitment to Human Values at Georgetown University or the History of Ideas tradition at The Johns Hopkins University. Nowhere is it clearer than in the pivotal role of the Great Books tradition at St. John's College in Annapolis and Santa Fe. But it also appears in whatever thematic unity a faculty has adopted, such as the focus on the Future of Humanity at the University of Oklahoma or the central orientation of Modern Studies at Loyola College in Maryland. In each case the program takes on a special emphasis or character from an outlook that is expressive of the institution. Taken together, these approaches bespeak the richness and variety of Graduate Liberal Studies within the commonalities that link the programs.

Finally, programs almost always include some integrative, summative or capstone element which brings the elements of the curriculum into harmony or synthesis with one another. Frequently this is a research thesis, major essay or other piece of work which the student undertakes independently of course work near the end of the program. The range of projects is as various as the students or the programs, but what the studies accomplish, in addition to examining their topics in depth, is to bring the whole course of study into focus. In other cases, the unifying element may be a capstone seminar in which participants are asked to relate their prior study to a common theme which is examined by the whole group. Yet in others, students may be asked to write reflective essays in which they consider the various parts of their study in relation to their personal goals in the program. From this examination they come to see the development of their own ideas. Whatever the device, the goal is synthesis of learning and the understanding of context.

It would be incorrect to assert that a program which lacked any of these charactristics was not a genuine Graduate Liberal Studies program. With as many offerings available as there are, no irreducible minimum will describe them all. But elements such as these are usually present, and among all the programs there is a definite sense of identity and distinctiveness from other offerings in the curriculum. Most often this distinctiveness is also represented by a separate administrative entity for the program.

These very distinctions of Graduate Liberal Studies programs have contributed to their success to date. There is an increasing recognition of the value of that which enhances humanness. It is this which is so attractive to mid-life adults whose focus and priority hitherto have been on the pragmatic and instrumental goals of getting started in careers, establishing families and otherwise defining themselves as adults in society. Participation in a Graduate Liberal Studies program is a process of both reaffirmation and self-discovery. It reaffirms because often Graduate Liberal Studies refreshes views, ideas and concepts that its students have heard at an earlier time. It involves self-discovery because it revisits familiar territory with new insight. Views, ideas and concepts that Graduate Liberal Studies students have heard at an earlier time take on a new significance. In other cases students may meet major works, issues and thinkers for the first time in ways that reveal new meaning to them. The value of a classic is that one can return to it with benefit regardless of one's age or maturity, in contrast to the airport or supermarket novels, whose purpose is to fill empty time and be thrown away. The same is true of great ideas and perennial issues of human life. The vitality of Graduate Liberal Studies lies in this renewal.

To make this reacquaintance or new discovery, nevertheless, does entail risk, as Charles Strain has pointed out in his essay. For this reason Graduate Liberal Studies students require an especial courage to embark on their programs. It is both exhilarating and exciting to expose one's accustomed habits of thought to challenge, as well as to re-enter the judgmental environment of an academic institution. I recall from years ago a University of Oklahoma graduate student who withdrew from the Graduate Liberal Studies program soon after entering because, he said, it had taken him years to build up the set of prejudices he operated with, and he did not want the program tampering with them. That fear (or, for some, that hope) points up the transforming character of education for adults. This is especially true of Graduate Liberal Studies programs because of the breadth of their scope, the fundamental character of their concerns and the profound thinking they ask their participants to undertake.

Along with these benefits to their participants, the programs also have great value to the institutions that conduct them. They often are the source of innovation and creativity that spread to other programs of the college or university. Teaching in this way rekindles the dedication of faculty members and affirms their own sense of self-esteem and worth. Instructors in the programs learn from each other and gain new insights. The president of one institution that offers a Graduate Liberal Studies program

139

commented recently that even if the program did not support itself, it would be valuable to maintain because of what it had done for the morale and development of its faculty.

Withal that, what does Graduate Liberal Studies have to look forward to in the future? In fact, the trends appear to be very promising, and Graduate Liberal Studies seems well attuned to needs for education that now are appearing.

Several years ago the dean of adult learning in the United States, Dr. Cyril O. Houle, addressed a conference on "The Liberal Arts College and the Experienced Learner." He described two previous ages in American higher education that had been marked first by a group of relatively small colleges with set curricula which moved younger students towards careers in the liberally educated professions, such as law, teaching, medicine, the ministry and landownership. This was followed by an era of research, specialization and professional education that was characterized by the elective system, credits, residency and degrees, all of which now have become familiar to us. He then foretold the emergence of a third era of higher education in which the education of young adults would be prominent, although altered in arrangements. More important he foresaw "a powerful thrust toward lifelong learning" with new patterns of degrees, a new family of credentials, new techniques for measuring academic accomplishments, and "a swelling number of middle-aged or older citizens who seek broader or more liberal forms of education."[1] Dr. Houle looked ahead about fifty years for the realization of this third era, but in fact it is already arriving.

Graduate Liberal Studies programs will soon encounter the interests of a rapidly expanding mid-life adult population. The numbers of persons from their late thirties to their fifties, sixties and even seventies who have found their way to Graduate Liberal Studies programs will soon be joined by the throngs of the post-war Baby Boom. The oldest of them are now entering their forties, and they, with their successors who were born as late as 1964, form the largest age cohort in our history. Their numbers alone have had major impact on our society as they have passed through each stage of life, and education programs for these mid-life adults will be no exception.

Not only is this group exceptional in its numbers. It is also exceptional in its character and educational composition. Because of the greatly increased opportunity for college and university education during the last generation, a much higher proportion of these young adults has already attained baccalaureate degrees than was ever true earlier in our history. Further, the recent pressure toward vocationalism and professionalism has left them bereft of the solid base of liberal education pursued by the majority of college graduates in the past. Unfortunately, and this has an important implication for Graduate Liberal Studies, they may also be weaker in the skills of reading and of written and spoken expression that liberal education usually nurtures. But all signs are that this already highly educated group will seek further education to a greater degree than did their predecessors.

It appears also that many of them recognize a gap in their liberal learning or yearn to carry further what they have already learned. Surveys of young adults a few years ago indicated that they were generally satisfied with their lives and their attainments, but over half felt they were inadequately prepared in the humanities. Whatever one thinks of the intellectual timbre of the recent jeremiads on American higher education, the controversy, interest and popularity of works such as William Bennett's *To Reclaim a Legacy*,[2] Alan Bloom's *The Closing of the American Mind*,[3] and E. D. Hirsch, Jr.'s *Cultural Literacy*[4] evince concern among large numbers of American adults over the adequacy of their cultural stock and understanding. Graduate Liberal Studies programs provide a means to turn the energy of this accusatory finger-pointing into satisfying and beneficial self-cultivation.

Happily the arrival of this horde of new adult learners also coincides with an emerging sensitivity to issues of adult development and the decision by many adults to choose education as a means of satisfying their ongoing needs. While studies about the change and evolution of adults' goals at various points in their lives differ on specifics, they have clearly challenged the notion of adulthood as a monolithic period. They have especially pointed up the need of mature adults for enrichment and exploration of values, once some of their other life tasks have been fulfilled. Again, this is a positive indicator for the future role of Graduate Liberal Studies.

Related to this is the important phenomenon of the lengthening of active life among our population. Some of the earlier adult-development literature points to the late fifties and sixties as a period of withdrawal and preparation for

141

retirement. Not so any longer. With the life expectancy for great numbers extending into the eighties and beyond, with compulsory retirement caps being taken off employment, and with physical and intellectual vigor sustained into the late seventies or later, many adults want to explore new opportunities. Many adult-related programs report an increased number of entrants past sixty who state that they want a "third career" or a new departure in a life that offers many more years of active involvement.

Graduate Liberal Studies faces an opportunity and challenge of a different sort from another sector of our population. Relatively few Graduate Liberal Studies programs enroll many members of minority groups. None of the programs is overtly discriminatory, and each would be aghast if any such suggestion were made. The absence of ethnic minorities is rooted in the same conditions that affect other aspects of our society and result in underrepresentation in those sectors as well. Yet the omission of these participants is undeniable and should give rise to concern. Have the programs sought adequately to attract persons from the growing numbers of well educated Blacks, Hispanics, Native Americans and Asians? Is there an ethnocentricity to the existing programs that makes them unattractive to persons of non-European descent? Can our interdisciplinarity be made intercultural as well? These questions and others do not lead to an easy solution, but they will become increasingly important for Graduate Liberal Studies in the future.

Beyond their appropriateness to the changing age and educational structure of our population, Graduate Liberal Studies programs address important intellectual needs in our society. We see a turning away from the extreme specialization that has marked the development of the disciplines in recent years. There is a demand for broader and more integrative perspectives within and between disciplinary study. Issues are being raised in context rather than in isolation, so that related circumstances and knowledge become necessary for understanding and solution. There is greater recognition of the interconnectedness of problems, not only within countries but throughout the world. Inquiry is becoming problem-oriented without regard for the academic or intellectual boundaries that previously limited investigation. There is a decline of confidence in positivistic scientism as a basis for knowledge and action, and a willingness to reintroduce value concerns into decision making. Above all, there is a search for community and human relationship. In considerable measure Graduate Liberal Studies programs foster study and understanding with regard to all of these concerns and will make a significant contribution in the future.

A recent study of the future university urges that faculty and institutions take a fresh look at their roles.[5] It emphasizes the need for strong grounding in the disciplines, but also for problem-oriented and multidisciplinary study that is aware of complex issues and the context of knowledge beyond the university. The authors have a different starting point from that usually assumed by Graduate Liberal Studies programs, but their exhortation is one to which Graduate Liberal Studies faculty and programs can respond.

Let me close by suggesting that the growing demand for education from already well educated adults and the special intellectual quality of Graduate Liberal Studies programs indicate the need for a doctoral degree characterized by Graduate Liberal Studies perspectives and approaches. The Association of Graduate Liberal Studies Programs has given consideration to such a model of study in the past, and a few member institutions have made preliminary explorations to establish such programs, but so far none has come into being. The Graduate Liberal Studies movement has now matured to a point where the creation of an advanced level of opportunity becomes a practicable goal.

If such a program were to be initiated, it should be characterized by the same traditions of quality and the same adaptability that our master's level programs have achieved. It should insist upon careful selection for admission, rigorous standards of performance in the educational content, adherence to the mission and guidelines of the sponsoring institution, and completion of a major individual work that would merit doctoral recognition. At the same time, the program should acknowledge the exigencies of the adult, and probably part-time, student in scheduling and pacing. Content should be interdisciplinary and integrative in orientation, although specific disciplinary study may at times be necessary to achieve that goal. Programs should be flexible in design and take their shape from planning that reflects student initiative as well as faculty direction. Measures of achievement and competence similarly should be attuned to the circumstances of the individual student. The major independent study should be a problem- or issue-oriented undertaking that demonstrates not only breadth of knowledge and creativity, but an ability to synthesize and integrate learning in a manner that makes a distinctive contribution.

Many leaders of Graduate Liberal Studies programs will recognize the desire among their graduates for such a program. They also receive overtures from students in other disciplines who wish to pursue Graduate Liberal Studies at a post-master's level. There is an emerging body of practice and intellectual understanding that characterizes Graduate Liberal Studies and which can give definition and substance to such a curriculum. The establishment of such programs would be an important addition to our academic resources at this time.

In sum, Graduate Liberal Studies has not only established an important new role for itself in the panoply of graduate education. It faces the possibility of playing an even greater role, both in numbers and in level. There are many opportunities for innovation in content and method. One is confident that those faculty who have already been so imaginative in creating the existing programs will rise to the new challenges.

William H. Maehl, Ph.D.
The Fielding Institute

Endnotes

1. John A. Valentine, "The Liberal Arts College and the Experienced Learner," *Adult Leadership* (February 1975), pp. 238-99.

2. William Bennett, *To Reclaim a Legacy* (Washington, D.C.: National Endowment for the Humanities, 1984).

3. Alan Bloom, *The Closing of the American Mind* (New York: Simon and Schuster, 1987).

4. E. D. Hirsch, Jr., *Cultural Literacy* (Boston: Houghton Mifflin Company, 1987).

5. Ernest A. Lynton and Sandra E. Elman, *New Priorities for the University* (San Francisco: Jossey-Bass, Inc., 1987), pp. 132-45.

CONTRIBUTORS

HERBERT A. ARNOLD is Professor of Letters and German Language and Literature at Wesleyan University. While completing his doctoral studies at Würzburg, he taught German language in Liverpool, in Würzburg and at Wesleyan, where he became a member of the faculty in 1963. Professor Arnold has chaired both of his departments, and has served six terms as director of Wesleyan's program in Heidelberg. He has written on a wide range of topics, including German history and historical theory, German literature and drama, as well as opera and popular song. He has translated several books on modern Germany and remains active in the Modern Language Association and in A.F.S.

WILLIAM M. CHACE is Vice Provost for Academic Planning and Development at Stanford University. A former Woodrow Wilson fellow, he holds an M.A. and Ph.D. in English from the University of California at Berkeley and a B.A. from Haverford College in Pennsylvania. As a Professor of English he won the Dean's Award for Excellence in Teaching and continues to teach courses on James Joyce, W. B. Yeats, and English literature since 1750. He has published numerous articles, anthologies and textbooks as well as two books of criticism: *The Political Identities of Ezra Pound and T. S. Eliot* (1973) and *Lionel Trilling: Criticism and Politics* (1980).

ANN COLUZZI is a teacher of English at the Duke Ellington School of the Arts, in the District of Columbia. A graduate of Trinity College, she received a Masters Degree in English and a Masters Degree in Liberal Studies at Georgetown University, where she is now a candidate for the advanced certificate in Liberal Studies. In 1983 Mrs. Coluzzi received an Independent Studies in the Humanities grant from the Council for Basic Education and the National Endowment for the Humanities, which she used to pursue research and to develop a textbook of Asian-Pacific mythology for students. She is now coordinator of Introduction to the Arts at the Duke Ellington School.

FRANK J. CUNNINGHAM is Assistant to the Provost and Associate Professor of Philosophy at Loyola College in Maryland. He received his B.S. in Biology from Fairfield University and his M.A. and Ph.D. in Philosophy from Fordham University. Subsequently, he was a Visiting Fellow and Associate Research Scientist in the Biology Department at The Johns Hopkins University. He is currently pursuing an M.S. in Biochemistry at the University of Maryland. He has published articles on Plato and on death of God theology. His present research interests center on process philosophy and molecular biology.

CAROL DAVIDOW received her Master of Arts in Humanities degree from Xavier University in 1985. She serves as Director for Schools for the Cincinnati Business Committee and as Manager of the Partners in Education Program for the Cincinnati Chamber of Commerce. A nationally known speaker and consultant on partnership programs between schools and businesses, she has contributed to several books on the subject published by university presses. She was chosen to be the 1988 recipient of the Friars' "Francis Award" for service to education and youth.

ALLIE FRAZIER is Professor of Philosophy at Hollins College, Virginia. A former president of the Association of Graduate Liberal Studies Programs (1981-85), he directed the Master of Liberal Studies program at Hollins for twelve years.

BARBARA GERBER received her doctorate from the University of Wisconsin, taught at St. Lawrence University from 1965 to 1973 and directed its Junior Year Abroad program in Rouen, France, from 1971 to 1972. In 1973, she joined the faculty of Brooklyn College, where she is currently Professor of Comparative Literature. From 1979 to 1981, she was the Executive Officer of the Special Baccalaureate Degree Program for Adults, and from 1981 to 1985 the director of all undergraduate Special Degree Programs for Adults. She initiated the M.A.L.S. program at Brooklyn College in 1981 and has served as its director since its inception. Active in the Association of Continuing Higher Education and the Association of Graduate Liberal Studies Programs, she has presented papers related to adult learners in non-traditional programs at national meetings of both these organizations, and in 1986 was a presenter for The Johns Hopkins University Seminars on Programs for Adult Learners sponsored

146

by the National Endowment for the Humanities.

CHARLES B. HANDS received his M.A. at the University of Pennsylvania and his doctorate at the University of Notre Dame. He has taught at the University of Notre Dame and at Loyola College in Maryland, where he is presently Professor of English. In addition to writing on Hawthorne, Melville, Frost, and other American authors, he designed, and still directs, the Master of Modern Studies program at Loyola. Active for the past ten years in the Association of Graduate Liberal Studies, he is presently Secretary of that organization.

DAVID B. HOUSE earned his doctoral degree in German studies from the University of Southern California in 1979. From 1981 through 1984 he served as director of the Master of Liberal Arts Program at USC. He has been Director of the Division of Arts and Sciences in the School of Continuing Studies at The Johns Hopkins University since 1984. He is currently writing a book on continuing liberal education, to be published next year.

BETTY COATS LINDSEY received her undergraduate education at Sullins College, Bristol, Virginia, and at the University of Alabama. A 1984 graduate of the Master of Arts in Liberal Studies program at the New School for Social Research in New York City, she is presently a doctoral candidate in English at the City University of New York and is preparing to write her dissertation on the novels of Conrad.

WILLIAM H. MAEHL is President of The Fielding Institute, an external professional doctoral program located in Santa Barbara, California. Formerly he was Professor of History, Vice Provost for Continuing Education and Public Service, and Dean of the College of Liberal Studies at The University of Oklahoma.

WILLIAM J. MEYER is one of the founding faculty of the Master of Liberal Studies program at The University of Michigan-Flint. He is presently the Director of Graduate and Special Programs and Associate Professor of Political Science at that institution. Professor Meyer received his doctorate from The Pennsylvania State University and his primary field is political philosophy. He is the author of *Public Good and Political Authority* and *The Political Experience*.

CHARLES R. STRAIN is Director of the Master of Arts in Liberal Studies Program and Associate Professor of Religious Studies at DePaul University, Chicago. He is the co-author of *Polity and Praxis* (1985), the co-editor of *Technological Change and the Transformation of America (1987)*, and the editor of the forthcoming *Prophetic Visions and Economic Realities.*